Terry P

111 Literary Places in London That You Shouldn't Miss

Photographs by Karin Tearle

111

emons:

To my friends Peter David (1951-2012) and Celia, adopted Londoners, for so many happy memories of Washington and London, and so much else.

MIX
Paper from responsible sources
FSC® C043106
FSC www.fsc.org

Layout: Editorial Design & Art Direction, Conny Laue, based on a design by Lübbeke | Naumann | Thoben
Maps: altancicek.design, www.altancicek.de
Basic cartographical information from Openstreetmap, © OpenStreetMap-Mitwirkende, OdbL
Editing: Martin Sketchley
Printing and binding: Grafisches Centrum Cuno, Calbe
Printed in Germany 2023
ISBN 978-3-7408-1954-5
First edition

Guidebooks for Locals & Experienced Travellers
Join us in uncovering new places around the world at www.111places.com

Foreword

London, rich in literature and literary associations, is full of surprising stories about the places where writers were born, died, lived and loved. They made the capital a backdrop for the plots and significant events in their books and in the lives of their characters.

The city's population in 1600, towards the end of the Elizabethan Era (1558-1603), was about 200,000, and it comprised little more than the Square Mile (the City of London) and small outlying villages. Yet it was a place where William Shakespeare, Edmund Spenser, Ben Jonson, and Christopher Marlowe flourished.

William Caxton brought the printing press to London in 1476 after having printed the first English-language book in the city of Bruges three years earlier. After Caxton's death in 1491, his German associate, appropriately named Wynkyn de Worde, moved the workshop to Fleet Street in 1500, the first printer on this small street that would become synonymous with printing and publishing.

De Worde was also the first to set up a book stall at St Paul's Churchyard, making this spot the centre of the book trade. Eventually, nearby Paternoster Row became home to many publishing houses but was later destroyed during the Blitz.

This book is about books, their writers, and the places they knew, as well as manuscripts, rare volumes, and the institutions that hold them. To walk the streets here is to experience layers of the past, for London is an architectural palimpsest, where new foundations have been built upon older ones through the centuries. It is also a palimpsest of history and literature. Readers will discover the real places from literary works across the city, one book, poem, and play at a time.

Terry Philpot

111 Literary Places

1 All Hallows by the Tower

Samuel Pepys records the Great Fire of London

On 2 September, 1666, Samuel Pepys was woken by his maid with news of the first day of the Great Fire of London. He went back to sleep. The next day matters were more alarming. The fire had started in a shop in Pudding Lane, and he recounts in his diary how, on the 5th, Elizabeth, his wife, woke him at 2am with 'new Cryes of "Fyre!"', for the conflagration had reached the church at the bottom of Seething Lane, where the couple lived. He removed Elizabeth, his manservant, and maid – and did not forget to take his gold – by boat to Woolwich, where they had sheltered from the plague a year earlier. There, he records, 'But Lord, what a sad sight by moonlight to see the whole City almost on fire – that you might see it plain at Woolwich, as if you were by it.'

By the time he returned home at 7am, he was surprised to see his house still standing, for houses were being blown up to make a fire-stop. However, the 'Dyall' and porch of the church he refers to as All Hallows, Barking, had been burned, and Pepys went up what he calls the steeple (the tower) 'and there saw the saddest sight of desolation I ever saw. Everywhere great fires. Olye [oil] cellars and brimstone and other things burning. I became afeared to stay there too long; and therefore down again as fast as I could, the fire being spread as fast as I could see it...'.

Hopes were reported that the fire had been stopped (as it was the next day) and Pepys went off to continue to observe the disaster in the city streets ('all in dust') and found homeless people camping in Moor Fields (Moorfields). The Royal Exchange was 'a sad sight'. He saw more devastation and glass melted and buckled 'like parchment' and a cat alive but with its hair burned off. That night, having lodged his staff, with food and drink, in his Navy Board office, he slept fitfully. The fire destroyed 3,200 homes and 87 parish churches.

Address Byward Street, EC3R 5BJ, +44 (0)207 481 2928, www.ahbtt.org.uk | Getting there Underground to Tower Hill (Circle and District lines); DLR to Tower Gateway | Hours See website for current information on visiting and services | Tip Pepys is buried in St Olave's Church and there is a bust of him in Seething Lane Garden, which connects the two churches (www.stolave.com).

2 Arnold Bennett's Steps

A novelist's ascent to fame

Arnold Bennett might have called his award-winning novel *Granville Place* (now Gwynne Place), but published in 1926, he chose the fictional *Riceyman Steps*. The steps, which lead from 'the noise, dust and dirt' of King's Cross Road, were, he wrote: 'twenty in number… divided by a half-landing into two series of ten'. They were known locally as Plum Pudding Steps until they were popularly renamed after the novel. Today the steps, once lined by tall houses, are straddled by a bland hotel, which replaced a car park, but they lead to a park, where formerly there was Bennett's Riceyman Square, in which once stood the grand church of St Philip.

Regarded as his best London novel (he was mainly famous for his dozen or so 'Potteries' novels and short stories), it is set in Clerkenwell, which Bennett visited many times for his research and read about extensively. His knowledge of antiquarian books is also evident, in what was his first attempt at what he called a novel of 'psychological realism'.

Bennett's Henry Earlforward is a miserly second-hand bookseller. The novel is a moral tale where greed and obstinacy destroy Earlforward and his wife, the widowed, comfortably-off former Mrs Violet Arb. Their situation contrasts with the life of their faithful but poor 23-year-old widowed maidservant Elsie Sprickett (a 'dowdy over-plump figure'), who represents life and the future, just as the bulbs cultivated at the steps, in this run-down place, offer hope. She is honest, self-sacrificing, loving, kind, simple and humble, and her everyday life is one of toil.

When Earlforward dies in front of his wife, the coverage in the evening newspapers – 'Mysterious death of a miser in Clerkenwell' – 'lifted Riceyman Steps to a height far above prize-fighting, national economies and the embroiled ruin of Europe'. Just as Bennett elevated obscure lives.

Address Gwynne Place, WC1X 9QE | **Getting there** Train or Underground to Kings Cross (Northern, Piccadilly, Hammersmith & City, Circle, and Metropolitan lines) | **Hours** Unrestricted | **Tip** The nearby Grant Museum of Zoology is one of Britain's oldest natural history museums, with 62,000 specimens from the animal kingdom (www.ucl.ac.uk/culture).

3 Athenaeum Club

Where two great writers reconciled

Charles Dickens (see ch. 19) and William Makepeace Thackeray (see ch. 96), two of the 19th century's greatest novelists, had an uneven relationship and quarrelled even when friends, but in 1863 they had not spoken for five years. Thackeray had made disobliging remarks about Ellen Ternan, now widely accepted to have been Dickens' lover. Also, Dickens' young friend, the journalist Edmund Yates, had disparaged Thackeray in an article in *Town Talk*. The older man complained to the committee of the Garrick Club, of which all three were members, that Yates had spied on him at the club. Yates was expelled and Dickens resigned in protest.

When Thackeray visited Dickens' daughter Kate and her husband, he expressed the view that it was 'ridiculous that he and her father… should be in a position of enmity toward one another', and Kate urged Thackeray to 'say a few words', as her father was 'more shy of speaking than you are'. But Dickens claimed to have taken the initiative in May. As he was hanging up his hat in the pilloried hall of the Athenaeum he saw Thackeray's haggard face and asked him whether Thackeray had been ill, and thus they were reconciled. Dickens, however, was not known for being the first to proffer the hand of friendship, having once said that 'quarrelling is all very well, but the making up is dreadful'.

In another account, the author of *Vanity Fair* was talking to Sir Theodore Martin, the Scottish writer, and Dickens passed nearby without any recognition of his former friend. Thackeray broke away and approached Dickens as the latter had his foot on the club's imposing staircase. Martin said that he saw Thackeray speak and hold out his hand to his former friend. They shook hands and exchanged a few words, and Thackeray went back to Martin, telling him, 'I am glad I have done this' or, 'I love that man, and I could not resist the impulse'.

Address 107 Pall Mall, SW1Y 5ER, +44 (0)207 930 4843, www.athenaeumclub.co.uk | **Getting there** Underground to Green Park (Piccadilly, Jubilee and Victoria lines) or Piccadilly Circus (Piccadilly and Bakerloo lines) | **Hours** Admission is to members only, but you can see the hall through the windows of the main door | **Tip** In nearby Piccadilly you'll find Albany, a discreet apartment block built in 1803, whose notable residents have included Edward Heath, Lord Byron, Graham Greene and William Gladstone.

4 Bank of England

Where The Wind in the Willows first stirred

By the time Kenneth Grahame had risen from the position of clerk at the Bank of England to be its secretary at the age of 39 in 1898, the Edinburgh-born writer was also a noted author of children's books, such as *The Pagan Papers* (1893) and *Dream Days* (1899). But his writing, especially *The Wind in the Willows*, was in part his retreat into a preferred imaginary world, one that represented an escape from his work – he called himself 'a clerk martyr' – an unsatisfactory marriage, and the world in which he lived.

There was another important source for his most famous novel, however. Grahame had married Elspeth Thomas in 1899, and their only child, Alastair, was born the following year. *The Wind in the Willows* derived from the bedtime stories about a toad and a rat he told Alastair, as he did in letters he would send later, when away escaping his marriage. Alastair must have taken all this to heart, for when he was six he was described as 'a baby who had swallowed a dictionary'. Those letters formed the first gentle breeze that eventually became *The Wind in the Willows*.

In 1903, shots were fired at Grahame in the bank; all missed, but the incident left him traumatised. This, his poor health and a relaxed approach to time keeping led to his departure in 1908, with a pension of £400. At this point, the family moved from London. His new freedom allowed him to devote himself to writing, and within the year *The Wind in the Willows* was published. He received no advance, and the book saw mixed reviews, however. Despite the initial lukewarm reaction, the story of the 'river-bankers', Mole, Ratty, Badger, Otter, and Mr Toad, sold well enough to give Grahame financial security and worldwide fame, having created one of the most imaginative, memorable and widely read stories of all time – one that delights and charms children and adults alike to this day.

Address Bartholomew Lane, EC2R 8AH, +44 (0)203 461 5545, www.bankofengland.co.uk | Getting there DLR or Underground to Bank (Central, District, Circle and Northern lines) | Hours Mon–Fri 10am–5pm and every third Thu 10am–7.30pm | Tip Founded in 1080, the present church of St Mary-le-Bow at Cheapside was built by Sir Christopher Wren at a cost of £15,000, with the third-highest spire of any Wren church. It is said that those born within the sound of its bells are Cockneys – true Londoners – not those born in Bow, east London.

5 Bedford Park

G. K. Chesterton's anarchists in arcadia

G. K. Chesterton set the opening of *The Man Who Was Thursday* in Bedford Park, said to be the world's first garden village, offering a rural life in an urban setting. He called it Saffron Park and gently mocks it. It is, he writes, 'as red and ragged as a cloud at sunset'. His is an artistic colony – as the actual Bedford Park was to an extent – that has not produced any definable form of art. It is a pleasant place, says Chesterton, with vague pretensions to be an intellectual centre. Its houses are in the Queen Anne style, but a stranger looking at these 'quaint houses' for the first time might think how oddly they are shaped, and thus 'how very oddly shaped' must be their inhabitants - 'artistic people on moderate incomes – to fit into them ... Nor when [the stranger] met the people was he disappointed in this respect'.

Bedford Park was an Arts and Crafts creation of the architect Norman Shaw, who also worked in Hampstead, some of whose architecture resembles that of Bedford Park. The novel came out in 1908, only 10 years after the community came into being. The origins of the two places, though, are different – one a planned community, the other a handsome suburb grown from a village.

The novel's Council of Seven Days heads a European anarchist group, each member named after a day of the week. The man who was Thursday is a local poet and police infiltrator, who attempts to foil an assassination in Paris. As well as Chestonian paradox, Chesterton, who converted to Catholicism 14 years later, sows Christian allegory into the book. Having suffered mild depression when at university (he was 34 when the book came out), he said that he wrote this book as an unusual affirmation that goodness and right were at the heart of every aspect of the world. Bedford Park, like later garden suburbs, too, grew from such progressive, optimistic beliefs.

Address Bedford Park, W4 | Getting there Underground to Turnham Green (District line) | Hours Always visible | Tip Chiswick House and Gardens, only a mile or so away, are stunning examples of 18th-century British architecture and landscaping, and spawned the English landscape movement, which influenced gardens from Blenheim Palace to New York's Central Park (www.chiswickhouseandgardens.com).

6 Bertrand Russell's Home

Nobel Prize winner's childhood at Pembroke Lodge

Built as a mole-catcher's lodge in around 1774, Pembroke Lodge is now a tearoom, and a wedding and banqueting venue. Set in 11 acres within Richmond Park, the York stone path, green lawns, manicured flower beds and handsome design betray its aristocratic past. In 1847 it was given by Queen Victoria to her Whig prime minister Lord John (later Earl) Russell. And in 1874, a two-year-old Bertrand Russell and his three-year-old brother Frank came here to live in the care of their grandparents, having been orphaned by the death of their parents, Lord and Lady Amberley.

Lord Russell died when Bertie was six, but the countess lived until he was an adult. From her he developed a deep religious faith – although he was later one of the century's great anti-religious polemicists – and a life-long love of English literature. Here, he imbibed an understanding of his family's role in British political history, and resistance to authority and tyranny that sowed his later dissent.

Frank went to Winchester, but Bertie was tutored at home, with an education that fitted the future prime minister that his grandmother aspired he should become. He learned modern languages, economics, constitutional history, science, and mathematics. A lonely child, Russell wandered in the grounds and woods, delighting in the changing seasons. But when he was 11 there came the great turning point in his intellectual life: he was introduced to Euclidean geometry. To him it was 'as dazzling as first love'.

Russell devoted his life to mathematics, philosophy, logic, and political activism. In 1950 he was awarded the Nobel Prize for Literature. In old age he reflected on the profound influence those long past years at Pembroke Lodge had had upon him: 'I grew accustomed to wide horizons and to an unimpeded view of the sunset. I have never since been able to live happily without both.'

Address Pembroke Lodge, Richmond Park, SW10 5HX, +44 (0)208 940 8207, www.pembroke-lodge.co.uk | Getting there Overground or Underground to Richmond (District line) | Hours Daily 10am–5pm | Tip You're in one of London's most extensive and attractive parks – look out for deer while you're there! 630 Red and Fallow deer have roamed freely here since 1637. They are wild, though, so keep 50 metres' distance!

7 The British Library

George the III's Library fit for a king

The tall glass tower that soars above the entrance hall of the British Library is home to the King's Library, the collection amassed by King George III during his 60-year reign. First housed in the Old Palace, Kew, this was one of the largest libraries in Europe when the king died in 1820. It held almost 64,000 printed books and 14,000 pamphlets, together with manuscripts, maps and topographical views dating from the mid-15th to the early-19th centuries.

After Kew, it was later moved to the Queen's House – where now stands Buckingham Palace. George's son, George IV, donated it to the British Museum in 1823, which doubled the museum's printed book collection. Between 1823 and 1827, a separate gallery – the King's Library – was built to store George III's books. Now the Enlightenment Gallery of the modern-day British Museum, it is the oldest room on the site. The library's subjects include history, geography, agriculture, military strategy, topography and literature in many European languages, as well as two complete first editions, in German, of the *Gutenberg Bible* and two first editions of Chaucer's *Canterbury Tales.*

During World War II, 124 volumes were destroyed, 304 were damaged beyond repair, and many others required substantial restoration. As a result, the collection was moved to the Bodleian Library at Oxford for the remainder of the war. Over the following decades, attempts were made to replace the lost works, but even today there are a few gaps. The collection returned to the British Library when it opened in 1997. George and his wife, Queen Charlotte, were great patrons of the arts, sciences and architecture, and during his 60 years on the throne he was a passionate book collector. The library rescues his reputation, which was overshadowed by his 'madness', and the loss of the American colonies.

Address 96 Euston Road, NW1 2DB, +44 (0)330 333 1144, www.bl.uk | Getting there Train, Overground or Underground to King's Cross (Victoria, Northern, Hammersmith & City and Circle lines) | Hours See website for opening of building and reading rooms (reader's ticket is required for the latter) | Tip A 10-minute walk south is the University of London's School of Oriental and African Studies, in which can be found the Brunei Gallery. Opened in 1996, it offers a changing programme of historical exhibitions from the Middle East, Asia and Africa (www.soas.ac.uk).

8 Brompton Cemetery

Where Beatrix Potter met Peter Rabbet

As a child Beatrix Potter would wander along the leafy paths of Brompton Cemetery near her home at 2 Bolton Gardens in prosperous South Kensington, where she had been born in 1886. There she saw the gravestones of Peter Rabbet [*sic*], Jeremiah Fisher, Susannah Nutkins, Mr Tod, Mr Brock, and Mr McGregor. The discovery of this connection only became possible when the 250,000 recorded burials in the cemetery, opened in 1840, were computerised. It's also possible that Potter knew a real Mr Nutkins – a butcher in nearby Gloucester Road.

Beatrix was born into a wealthy, Unitarian, middle class family. Both parents were the beneficiaries of Lancashire cotton fortunes, and neither had any cause to work, although Rupert Potter, a qualified barrister, did so until inheriting his wealth in 1883. Beatrix said that she could not remember a time when she did not try to invent pictures of a fairyland of wildflowers, animals, mosses and woods. She and her younger brother Bertram collected animals, beetles, dead birds, frogs and hedgehogs on which they 'experimented'. From this grew Beatrice's 'picture letters', often about her later familiar characters, the first sent to the son of her former governess.

When two publishers brought out some of her pictures as cards, she turned for advice to a family friend, Canon Hardwicke Rawnsley, an author and co-founder of the National Trust, about publishing a book. Being rejected by several publishers, she privately published *The Tale of Peter Rabbit* in 1901, her first step to transforming her animal characters into a series of best-selling books. As a result, Frederick Warne, publisher of children's titles, offered to bring out the book if the drawings were in colour. The book appeared in 1902. She then published a book a year until 1913, and then almost as frequently for the next 29 years until her death, aged 77, in 1943.

TOM WILLIAM NUTKINS
GRANDSON OF THE ABOVE,
WHO DIED JUNE 26TH 1906
AGED 14 YEARS.
ALSO OF
GEORGE NUTKINS
WHO ENTERED INTO REST
DECEMBER 24TH 1915
IN HIS 62ND YEAR.
HELEN NUTKINS

Address Fulham Road, SW10 9UG | Getting there Underground (District line) or Overground to West Brompton, or Earl's Court (District, Circle, and Piccadilly lines) | Hours Daily 7am–6pm | Tip Fulham Place on Bishop's Avenue is a short walk away. Once home of the bishops of London, visitors can take a tour to enjoy the glories of the palace and the magnificent 13-acre walled garden.

9 Browning Room

The Secret Wedding of Barrett and Browning

Only two witnesses – his cousin and her maid – attended one of the most famous of literary marriages: that of the poets Elizabeth Barrett and Robert Browning, at St Marylebone Church on 12 September, 1846. The secret ceremony is commemorated in the church's Browning Room, with a stained glass window, their wedding certificate, copies of their books and other memorabilia. In 2006, a *bas relief* of Elizabeth, matching one of Robert, was unveiled to mark the 160th anniversary of the marriage.

Their relationship began when Elizabeth, one of the most famous poets of the day, publicly praised Robert's poems, and he wrote to express his gratitude. She would not meet him, fearing he would see an 'ageing' invalid confined to her sofa: at 40, she was six years his senior. She finally allowed him to visit 50 Wimpole Street on 20 May, 1845. He fell in love with her, but when he sought marriage she feared her father, who had forbidden his children to marry. But by November, after more letters and visits, and realising that her father was a tyrant, she accepted his proposal.

While Robert was financially dependent on his parents, Elizabeth had inherited capital bringing in £350 a year. He agreed that they would live on her money in Italy, believed to be good for her health, but her will must leave her wealth to her siblings. A week later, accompanied by her dog and Wilson, her maid, the couple left secretly, arriving in Italy on 14 October. Florence was their home for the rest of their married life. They travelled widely, including several times to London, but never met her father.

Despite several miscarriages, in 1849 Elizabeth gave birth to a son, Pen. Robert left Florence for the last time in 1861, the year of Elizabeth's death, returning with Pen to live in London. Elizabeth is buried in Florence, while Robert rests in Poets' Corner, Westminster Abbey (see ch. 68).

Address St Marylebone Church, Marylebone Road, NW1 5LT, +44(0)207 563 1389, www.stmarylebone.org | **Getting there** Underground to Marylebone (Bakerloo line) or Baker Street (Bakerloo, Hammersmith & City, Circle, Metropolitan, and Jubilee lines) | **Hours** See website for current information on visiting | **Tip** Nearby Wigmore Hall is less well known than other London musical venues, but is one of the world's great concert halls, specialising in chamber and instrumental music, early music and song (www.wigmore-hall.org.uk).

10 Brown's Hotel

Kipling's Home from Home

Rudyard Kipling's long association with Brown's began with his honeymoon there with his American bride Caroline ('Carrie') in 1892, before embarking on a tour of America. When they went to check out, they were surprised to find that their bill of £22 had already been paid: an unexpected wedding present by the hotel.

The Nobel Prize winner and author of the *Just-So Stories* and *The Jungle Book* – which was written at Brown's Hotel – visited many times with Carrie, always using the same suite. Indeed, they spent much of the First World War there, during which their 18-year-old son John was killed at the Battle of Loos. They never had a London residence, as they owned the Jacobean manor of Bateman's in Sussex, and Kipling claimed Carrie could never cope with keeping two homes.

In December 1935 the couple were again at Brown's, where Kipling was revising his autobiography and his will. At the same time, his cousin, the prime minister Stanley Baldwin, had failed to win Cabinet backing for a deal with the French (which Kipling supported) by Sir Samuel Hoare, the Foreign Secretary, to give Mussolini's Italy a free hand in the subjugation of Ethiopia. This led to Hoare's resignation. Kipling's biographer, Andrew Lycett, says the news 'had a curious effect' on his subject. On 18 December Kipling wrote a poem on the pact and sent it to *The Times*. The next day he urgently sought that the newspaper return the poem, however, perhaps fearing it would embarrass Baldwin.

During another stay at Brown's Hotel in January, again to discuss his will, Kipling suffered a burst ulcer and was rushed to the nearby Middlesex Hospital. Lady Milner, wife of colonial administrator Alfred Milner, went to the hotel to comfort Carrie, who had spent the night with her husband, but Kipling died on 18 January, the couple's wedding anniversary, and two weeks past Kipling's 71st birthday.

Address Albemarle Street, W1S 4BP, +44 (0)207 493 6020, www.browns@roccofortehotels.com | Getting there Underground to Green Park (Piccadilly, Jubilee and Victoria lines) | Hours Open 24 hours | Tip Along Piccadilly, at the entrance arch to the Royal Academy, there's a red Grade II-listed original red telephone box, created by the architect Sir Giles Gilbert Scott in 1924.

11 Buck's Club

Inspiration for P. G. Wodehouse

A drone bee is one that does not work; appropriate, then, that in many of his Jeeves and Wooster and Blandings Castle novels and short stories, P. G. Wodehouse invented his Drones Club: a gentleman's club in Mayfair, largely based on the elegant Buck's in that part of London. Several of his characters, usually young, rich, idle, sometimes titled but always well-connected, are associated with the club. The disaster-prone Bertie Wooster's manservant, Jeeves, who is a member of another club appropriate to his class, earned his job when he introduced his master to raw egg as a hangover cure.

Drones Club members include Freddie Widgeon and Bingo Little. Other Wodehousian characters, equally comically ridiculous, are Monty Bodkin, Freddie Threepwood, and PSmith, who call each other 'Old Bean' or 'Old Crumper'. Wodehouse's clubs are affectionate, innocent parodies that were dated even when he created them.

Club members wear a 'rich purple' tie and run annual competitions, such as the golf tournament, squash handicap, and Fat Uncles Sweep. For the latter, the members bring their 'fat uncles' to the club to have their weight estimated for a jackpot prize by McGarry, the barman, who has a knack for this. The author's characters often speak in an upper class slang, using words such as 'drat' (a nuisance), 'nosebag' (food), 'toodle-oo' (goodbye), 'bracer' (a reviving drink), 'map' (face), and 'gruntled' (satisfied, that is, not disgruntled).

The club is a short walk from Bertie's fictitious home at 3 Berkeley Mansions, Berkeley Square. It's more like a public school with no masters, no lessons and continuous games. It's here, said Wodehouse, that 'to attract a fellow's attention you heave a bit of bread at him'. It was perhaps typical of Wodehouse, who is regarded as one of the greatest comic novelists, that he disliked clubs, even though he was a member of half a dozen.

Address Clifford Street, W1S 3RF, +44 (0)207 734 2337, www.bucksclub.co.uk | Getting there Underground to Piccadilly (Piccadilly and Bakerloo lines) | Hours Club open to members and guests only | Tip The nearby Wallace Collection, assembled by four generations of the Hertford family and bequeathed to the government in 1897, includes Rembrandt, Titian, Goya, Reynolds and Gainsborough in 25 galleries (www.wallacecollection.org).

12 Cadogan Hotel

The humiliation of being Oscar

The hotel is a symbolic watershed in the life of Oscar Wilde, for here his dazzling public life ended when, on 6 April, 1895, he was arrested. The unstable Marquess of Queensbury, father of Wilde's lover, Lord Alfred 'Bosie' Douglas, had left a note for Wilde at his club accusing him of 'posing as a somdomite [sic]'. Wilde, arguably unwisely, sued him for criminal libel, and lost. Though Wilde's illegal clandestine life had been revealed, he ignored the pleas of friends, immediately after the trial, to flee to the continent. Instead, he took a carriage to the Cadogan Hotel, where Douglas had been staying. Wilde was by then at the height of his fame and on the way he may have seen his name being removed from playbills in The Haymarket and the St James's Theatres.

Wilde sat and waited with Douglas and another friend, Robert Ross, drinking hock and seltzer. At 6.30pm, while Douglas had gone to the House of Commons to see a cousin who was an MP about the possibility of Wilde's prosecution, there was a knock at the door of room 118. One of two plain clothes policemen greeted the playwright with, 'Mr Wilde, I believe?' He was taken to Scotland Yard and charged with 'committing acts of gross indecency with other male persons', and then spent a night in custody in Bow Street police station and then Holloway to await the committal proceedings.

Wilde received two years' hard labour, and suffered disgrace and humiliation. The Cadogan Hotel was only 20 minutes' walk from Wilde's home at 34 Tite Street, where he lived with his wife Constance and two sons, Vyvyan and Cyril. Constance changed her and the children's surnames to a family name of Holland, and moved to Switzerland; Wilde never saw any of them again. On release, he went into exile in Italy and France. He died in the Hotel d'Alsace in Paris in 1900, and is buried at Père Lachaise Cemetery.

Address 75 Sloane Street, SW1X 9S9, +44 (0)207 048 7141, www.belmond.com | Getting there Underground to Sloane Square (District and Circle lines) | Hours 24 hours | Tip The National Army Museum, just a short distance away, shows the history of British land forces post-1914, through the stories of regiments and corps (www.nam.org).

13 Cambridge Circus

Where spies came out from the cold

John Le Carré named his MI6 headquarters The Circus after its fictional home in Cambridge Circus, where the service is said to have been located from 1945 onwards. The ground floor of the south-west corner is now a fast food outlet, but in Le Carré's fiction, Smiley and senior staff were housed on the top floor, while other officers were below. From this red-brick, turreted Edwardian building, MI6 agents are directed, operating throughout the USA, the UK and Europe as they seek to best Smiley's East European rival, Karla, head of the Moscow Centre – otherwise known as the KGB.

Le Carré's world is one of bluff and counter-bluff, agents and double agents, strange loyalties and betrayal, suspicion and ambivalence. In Le Carré's masterpiece *Tinker, Tailor, Soldier, Spy*, all of this is key to the plot, as there is a traitor in the midst of the service – a 'mole'. Smiley, who had been forcibly retired from his senior job in counter-intelligence, is brought back to the Circus to investigate, and uncover one of five suspected senior intelligence officers. They are identified by characters from the jingle: 'Tinker, tailor, soldier, sailor, rich man, poor man, beggarman, thief'. Smiley himself is a suspect – 'beggarman' – and must work covertly.

Smiley, a character who appears in eight of Le Carré's novels, is the very opposite of Ian Fleming's handsome James Bond, who is at home in society, glamorous but implausible, even before the films offered their elaborations. Smiley, by contrast, is self-effacing, middle-aged, small, portly, and bespectacled, a cuckold, a linguist, and a bibliophile. He and his work are depicted with all the detail and authority of the spy that Le Carré (as David Cornwell) had himself been, after becoming an MI5 officer in 1958. But the Smiley novels are also 'state of the nation' works, as Britain and the service seek to come to terms with the post-imperial world.

Address 138 Shaftesbury Avenue, WC2H 8HB | Getting there Underground to Leicester Square (Northern and Piccadilly lines) or Tottenham Court Road (Central, Elizabeth and Northern lines) | Hours Smiley's offices are the floors above the fast food café, and viewable from outside only | Tip A few minutes' walk away in Covent Garden you'll find St Paul's, 'the actors' church', where funeral and memorial services are held for actors. The walls are adorned with plaques that highlight this rich and unusual theatrical history.

14 Campden Grove

James Joyce ties the knot

It took 23 years and two children to do it, but in 1931 James Joyce and his muse, Nora Barnacle, married. It was only from early May to early September 1931 that they lived in a flat in 28 Campden Grove, and in July formalised their relationship in the now demolished register office on Marloes Road. It was nine years after his novel *Ulysses* had gained Joyce fame and notoriety (banned in Britain until 1936) and he was writing *Finnigan's Wake.*

The wedding was never going to be a quiet one, for there was great press interest that Joyce shunned. He eventually put out a statement that the couple had been invalidly wed in Austria in 1904, so the British marriage was 'for testamentary reasons'. But on the morning of the wedding there was widespread media coverage and the couple – he was 49 and of 'independent means', and she 47 – drew a veil over two decades of 'living in sin' by declaring themselves bachelor and spinster on the marriage certificate. They had two children and their daughter Lucia also was not best pleased, believing that her parents were already married. Nora's family in Galway disowned the couple.

Failing sight caused Joyce to become more dependent on Nora. She was never intimidated by his literary fame – she refused to read *Ulysses* and her response to his celebrity was to say to friends, 'I've always told him he should give up writing and take up singing'. She disparaged the seeming incomprehensibility of *Finnigan's Wake.* They lived in Paris throughout the 1930s, but the marriage of their son Giorgio and the birth in 1932 of a grandson, Stephen James, was no compensation for the severe mental illness that afflicted Lucia. The Nazi invasion of France forced the family to move back to Switzerland in 1939, leaving Lucia in an asylum in Brittany. A month later Joyce died of a perforated ulcer, and he now rests in a cemetery in Zurich.

Address 28 Campden Grove, W8 4JQ | Getting there Underground to High Street Kensington (Circle and District lines) | Hours Always visible from outside only | Tip Take the bus to Hyde Park Corner to visit the imposing Wellington Arch, which marks Wellington's defeat of Napoleon; take a lift to the roof for a good view of London.

15 Canonbury Tower

Oliver Goldsmith flees debtors

Oliver Goldsmith moved to Canonbury Tower for 18 months in 1762, to escape the temptations of inns and gambling nearer to his home in London. It was the home of his friend, bookseller and newspaper owner John Newbery. By this time the building, where the philosopher Francis Bacon once lived, had been converted into apartments, and Goldsmith's room was on the upper floors.

Though Goldsmith was said not to be a good reader, he would read books and his own poems to Newbery's nephew, Francis, who was interested in literature and music. Goldsmith, ever impecunious, arranged that Newbery should take care of his budget, when he came to the slow realisation that he was unable to take charge of his own finances. In return, he offered his journalistic services, for example writing prefaces. Newbery seems not to have realised what an exceptional talent he had secured at such low cost. It was an amicable relationship, which included Goldsmith's later employment of Francis.

In Goldsmith's time the tower was Canonbury House, built in the 16th century for the canons of the priory of St Bartholomew, but seized for Henry VIII by Thomas Cromwell. The writer seemed content in his residence: the large and handsome rooms, with their panels and plasterwork, made an ideal setting for his work, particularly given the lack of temptation. A local woman, Elizabeth Fleming, looked after his practical needs, from his bedtime drink to sewing his stockings. She would also make him small loans – for example 10d (5p) on 24 May, 1764. For relaxation he had a garden, tearooms on the nearby banks of the New River, and a quality of air such that it attracted Londoners up the hill at weekends. Goldsmith wrote *The Traveller, or a Prospect of Society*, in Canonbury Tower. In recognition of Newbery's help and friendship, Goldsmith gave warm tribute to him in his novel *The Vicar of Wakefield*.

Address 6 Canonbury Place, N1 2NY | Getting there Train, DLR and Underground to Highbury & Islington (Victoria line) | Hours By tour only on fourth Wed and second Fri of the month; see www.islingtonguidedwalks.com/our-walks | Tip The Estorick Collection of Modern Italian Art is the UK's only gallery devoted to modern Italian Art, and best known for its Futurist works (www.estorickcollection.com).

16 Carlyle's House

The French Revolution written here

Facing the stairs on the first floor of the graceful 300-year-old Carlyle's House is the drawing room where the great Scottish historian and cultural critic Thomas Carlyle wrote his major work, *The French Revolution*. The three volumes were published in 1837 (revised in 1857) but not before the original manuscript was accidentally burned by the maid of the philosopher John Stuart Mill, forcing the author to start from scratch. The book, still in print, was written with an unusual passion for historical works of the time, enhanced by Carlyle sometimes using the present tense. In this house he also wrote biographies of Cromwell and Frederick the Great, and his history of Chartism. His work had an influence on the novelist Charles Dickens (see ch. 19) and the critic John Ruskin.

Carlyle and his wife, Jane, also had an attic study built as a new top floor. This was intended to be a silent haven, but proved to be the least quiet room in the house. His work had him dubbed 'the sage of Chelsea' and earned him a statue on the Embankment. The house has a small garden, which both Carlyles cultivated, and where they relaxed with their dog, Nero.

The Carlyles rented the small, red-brick house (then No. 5) in 1834 for £34 a year. By design, Jane, herself an accomplished writer, ran the home on a limited budget, and so they rarely entertained. Both were known as great conversationalists, however, which also drew people such as the poets Robert Browning (see ch. 9) and Alfred Tennyson, the novelists Mrs Gaskell and George Eliot (see ch. 100), who lived nearby at 4 Cheyne Walk. In 1866, much to his own surprise, Carlyle was elected rector of Edinburgh University, against Benjamin Disraeli, the former prime minister (see ch. 82). Three days later, Jane died during a carriage ride in Hyde Park. Carlyle died in 1882, and is buried in Scotland.

Address 24 Cheyne Row, SW3 5HL, +44 (0)207 352 5108, www.nationaltrust.org.uk | Getting there Underground to Sloane Square (Circle and District lines), or South Kensington (Circle and District lines), then a 15-minute walk from each | Hours Wed 11am–4.30pm; pre-booked tours only | Tip Chelsea Physic Garden at 66 Royal Hospital Road was opened on four acres in 1673 by the Apothecaries Company to grow medicinal plants. It is now one of the most intimate, varied and horticulturally interesting of public gardens.

17 Cecil Court

Arthur Ransome's early workplace

Arthur Ransome, later to find fame as the author of *Swallows and Amazons*, came to London when he was 18, after an unhappy time at Rugby, and having abandoned his chemistry studies at university. Focussed on a literary career, he found lodgings in Clapham and a job as a general dogsbody with the publisher Grant Richards in Leicester Square, for pay of eight shillings (40p) a week. His intention, and that of his new employer, was that he should start at the bottom and rise to be a publisher. At lunchtime, he would often browse the bookshops in nearby Cecil Court and those – more in evidence then than now – along Charing Cross Road.

Came the man, came the part: he wrote that he had 'become intoxicated by the smell of the books fresh from the binders, and of the great stacks of printed sheets fresh from the printers that seemed to fill every floor of Mr Richards' offices'. But despite such 'intoxication', after six weeks he found a job at 7 Cecil Court as assistant to Ernest Oldmeadow, 'a short, stout, beady-eyed little man', and the eccentric owner of the financially unstable Unicorn Press, publisher of poetry and beautifully illustrated art books. His pay rose to £1. Oldmeadow, he recorded, had good intentions and a degree of success, but the company was supported only by 'very thin financial ice'. Employed, as he said, 'to do nothing', Ransome had stepped from the busy tide of Grant Richards 'into a quiet, almost stagnant backwater'. This gave him ample time for reading, and writing stories for the press.

His first holiday since leaving school was perhaps the most significant journey he ever took – he went to Coniston, in the Lake District, 'to the enchanted North', scene of his most famous novel. On return, he resigned from Unicorn Press, able now to live as an eventually successful freelance author and journalist, reporting the Russian Revolution.

Address WC2N 4EZ, www.cecilcourt.co.uk | Getting there Underground to Leicester Square (Northern and Piccadilly lines) | Hours Shops' times differ, but Cecil Court is open 24 hours | Tip Charing Cross Road, off Cecil Court, was not so long ago the centre of London's second-hand book trade. Sadly, few such bookshops remain, but those still open offer plenty of bargains, from antiquarian books to modern first editions – some signed.

18 The Charing Cross Hotel

Edith Wharton's passion changes her life

Edith Wharton endured many years of a loveless marriage to a husband 12 years her senior, in a relationship that made her ill. She came from an old, wealthy New York family, but her childhood was unhappy, too. Remarkably, though, by 1907, then aged 45, she had written three novels, including *The House of Mirth.*

The following year she began a three-year affair with Morton Fullerton, a promiscuous bisexual journalist and author who had little commitment. Wharton experienced a roller-coaster of emotions as they would meet, but Fullerton would then disappear to engage in other relationships. To escape scandal and servants' prying eyes, when they came over from France in 1909, they checked into Room 92, which had two bedrooms and a sitting room, at what was then the Charing Cross Hotel.

Here, the 47-year-old author became 'a sensual heroine', enjoying hitherto unknown love-making. As Fullerton left for America, Wharton was expressing her feelings in her 52-line erotic poem, 'Terminus' – a title indicating both her experience at the hotel and Fullerton again leaving her. Her affair was one where, she admitted, 'I have drunk the wine of love to the last… I have been warmed through and through, never to grow quite cold again, until the end.' Now she was able to write of love from heady personal experience.

In 1913, the Whartons divorced after 28 years of marriage. Edith moved to live in France permanently, where she continued to write novels. Indeed, in 1920 she was the first woman to win the Pulitzer Prize, for *The Age of Innocence*. She also created beautiful gardens, developed deep friendships, and became a renowned hostess. For her work for her adopted country with children and refugees during the First World War, Edith Wharton was decorated by the French government. Without the Charing Cross Hotel, much of this might not have happened.

Address The Clermont Hotel, The Strand, WC2N 5HX, +44 (0)207 523 5052, www.theclermont.co.uk | **Getting there** Underground to Charing Cross (Northern and Bakerloo lines), to Embankment (Bakerloo, Northern, Circle, and District lines) or train to Charing Cross | **Hours** Open 24 hours | **Tip** The Georgian church of St Martin's in the Fields, complete with balconies and box pews, is just steps away in Trafalgar Square. It's an architectural gem that holds frequent concerts, has a café, and is famous for its work with homeless people.

19 Charles Dickens Museum

Portrait of the writer as a young man

What happened to Margaret Gillies' portrait of 31-year-old Charles Dickens after it was last seen in 1886 is a mystery. So, too, is how it came to turn up again in 2017 – in South Africa. How did it get there?

It's likely that Dickens and the Scottish painter came to know one another through a shared interest in social reform. In 1843, Dickens wrote to Gillies and told her that he would turn up for a sitting the next day, 24 October, nearly two months before *A Christmas Carol* was published. The watercolour and gouache on ivory miniature was shown the following year at the Royal Academy. Nearly 40 years later, though, Gillies, wrote in a letter, held by the museum, that she could not account for the portrait, and had 'lost sight of it', which suggests unexplained loss. The only visual evidence of it was a simple black and white engraving. However, a house clearance in Pietermaritzburg revealed it in a box of trinkets. It was probably taken to South Africa by one of the sons of George Henry Lewes, lover of the novelist George Eliot (see ch. 100), when he emigrated there in the 1860s. The portrait, missing for 130 years, underwent extensive conservation, and is now in the museum after a fund-raising campaign.

The museum, situated in one of only three of Dickens' homes still standing (the other two are not in London), was where the novelist lived with his wife, Catherine, and their then three children, from March 1837 to December 1839. While here, Dickens wrote *Oliver Twist* and *Nicholas Nickleby,* completed *The Pickwick Papers,* and worked on *Barnaby Rudge*. The house was mainly used as a boarding house when the family left. In 1923, the Dickens Fellowship purchased it, and it was opened to the public in 1925. Today the house is home to over 100,000 items comprising furniture, personal effects, paintings, prints, photographs, letters, manuscripts, and rare editions.

Address 48 Doughty Street, WC1N 2LX, +44 (0)207 405 2127, www.dickensmuseum.com | Getting there Underground to Russell Square (Piccadilly line) | Hours Wed – Sun 10am – 5pm | Tip The Foundling Museum was once part of the Foundling Hospital or orphanage, which encompassed Coram Fields, now in front of the building; it outlines the history of the orphanage in the context of children's welfare at that time (www.foundlingmuseum.org.uk).

20 Christ Church

Jack London in the Abyss

Jack London was 25 when he came to London's East End in 1902 to write about poverty in what became perhaps his most famous book, *The People of the Abyss*. Published the next year, when he also found fame with his third novel, *The Call of the Wild*, this was his personal favourite. For the book, he dressed shabbily, passing himself off as a seaman. In a grey and drab city he slept in cramped lodgings, sometimes sharing a room, and casual wards, a night's bed and breakfast paid for by backbreaking work. He wrote to friends, 'I've read of misery, and seen a bit; but this beats anything I could even have imagined.' This was a sickening 'human hell-hole'.

Arriving on 6 August, the American completed the book in seven weeks, after visiting people's homes, joining queues in soup kitchens, and observing workshops and the unemployed. One of the few places he names is the churchyard of Nicholas Hawksmoor's majestic English baroque Christ Church in Spitalfields, where he tells of 'a sight I never wish to see again'. The garden in the church's shadow was small and flowerless, with sharp-spiked railings – which it still has – to stop the homeless bedding down for the night. He and two companions encountered a homeless woman, with her possessions in two bulky bundles. Either side of the gravel path were 'a mass of miserable and distorted humanity ... a welter of rags and filth, of all manner of loathsome skin diseases ... and bestial faces', most of whom slept during the afternoon as they were unable to by night. A baby, with no pillow or covering, slept on a hard bench with no one to look after it.

London set the tone for later fly-on-the-wall coverage of poverty with his use of graphic reportage, newspaper cuttings, official tables and statistics detailing nutrition and work, and polemic. All showed (literally) crippling poverty, sweatshops, aimlessness, and squalor.

Address Commercial Street, E1 6LY, +44 (0)207 377 2440, www.ccspits.org | Getting there Underground to Aldgate East (Hammersmith & City and District lines) | Hours See website for current information on visiting | Tip A striking mural on St George's Town Hall on Cable Street commemorates the Battle of Cable Street in 1936, when a march through the largely Jewish area by Oswald Mosley's Blackshirts was seen off by barriers and force by Jewish, socialist, Irish and other opponents.

21 Clapham Common

Graham Greene's art imitated his life

In Graham Greene's 1951 novel *The End of the Affair*, Maurice Bendrix, the narrator, an unmarried novelist, lives on what was then socially the 'wrong side – the south side – of the Common', while his married lover, Sarah Miles, lives on the north side. In 1935, Greene, fresh from Liberia to write his *Journey without Maps*, moved with his wife and two children from Oxford to the handsome Queen Anne house at 14 Clapham Common North Side. When the house was seriously damaged by war-time bombing during the family's absence, it gave Greene the idea for a decisive moment in the novel, when Bendrix's house is similarly bombed. The novel rehearses Greeneian themes of deception and jealousy. But in this critical incident, the Catholic Greene also explores the mercy of God, as he had in *Brighton Rock, The Power and the Glory,* and *The Heart of the Matter.*

The End of the Affair takes place during and just after the war, and the Common is the principal location for some scenes, with the action moving from the south to the north side. When Bendrix goes to a party at Sarah's house and slips out for a walk across the Common with her cuckolded husband, Henry, a civil servant, Greene lyrically evokes an oasis of calm in war-time. Parts of the book take in other local places: the Pontefract Arms (now The Windmill) on Clapham Common South Side, and St Mary's Catholic Church in Clapham Park Road, but it also moves to central London with Corpus Christi Church and Rules restaurant, both in Maiden Lane, Covent Garden.

The novel also partly reflects Greene's own affair with Catherine Walston, a wealthy married American, which began in 1946 and lasted until the 1960s. In the early stages of that relationship, he was still married to his wife, Vivien (whom he never divorced), but living in London with Dorothy Glover, and with possibly another lover in Paris. The novel is dedicated to 'C'.

Address 14 Clapham Common North Side, SW4 0RF | Getting there Underground to Clapham Common (Northern line) | Hours Common unrestricted; house viewable from outside only | Tip The Common's magnificent bandstand, erected in 1890, is Grade II-listed and the largest in London (www.londongardenstrust.org).

22 Cloth Fair

John Betjeman's love nest

The first and second floors and small roof terrace of this modest Georgian house were John Betjeman's London home for nearly two decades. While his wife, the horse-loving Penelope, lived in the country, he did not want to share with friends in London. A flat for himself would be convenient for work, and also enable him to continue his long-lasting relationship with the aristocratic Lady Elizabeth Cavendish, whom he met in 1951. Early on she distanced herself from Betjeman, not wanting to break up his marriage, but they became closer, and in later years would often take holidays together or with others in Europe.

Betjeman lived at 43 Cloth Fair from 1954 to 1973, although he moved out from 1958 to 1959 after severe fire damaged the house. In 1960, his verse autobiography, *Summoned by Bells,* cemented his fame as Britain's best known and most popular of poets, while he became Poet Laureate in 1972. This was also an area whose buildings, alleys and passages appealed to his architectural and historical tastes. When in 1977 he spoke of why he loved living there, it was with a touch of very Betjemanian romantic evocation: '... because everything could be reached on foot, down alleys and passages. Like all county towns it had a bit of every trade ... On some weekly nights there was bell-ringing from the tower of St Bartholomew's the Great, just such bells as the walled city must have heard when there were 108 churches in its square mile. Behind me was Smithfield Market with its Chaucerian characters and Medieval-looking barrows'.

Despite the area's gentrification, visitors today will appreciate his words. But after the development of the Brutalist Barbican estate, which towered over the Clerkenwell skyline, Betjeman moved to his last London home in Radnor Walk, Chelsea. He died in 1984 at his country home in Cornwall, with Lady Elizabeth at his side.

Address 43 Cloth Fair, EC1A 7JQ | Getting there Train or Underground to Farringdon (Elizabeth, Hammersmith & City, and Metropolitan lines) | Hours Viewable from outside 24 hours; apartment available for holiday lets via Landmark Trust (www.landmarktrust.org.uk) | Tip Walk to St John's Lane to visit St John's Gate; this Tudor gatehouse and parts of the 12th century church are reminders of the Priory of the Knights of St John, a forerunner of St John's ambulance; a museum tells its history.

23 C. L. R. James' Last Home

The cricketing radical

C. L. R. James (never Cyril Lionel Robert) first went to Nelson in Lancashire in 1932 from his native Trinidad, but died in 1989, aged 88, in the small, book-filled flat above this building in Brixton, at the centre of London's Afro-Caribbean community. In between times he was a revolutionary, novelist, historian, literary critic, philosopher, and political analyst. In the eyes of many, he was the foremost writer on cricket. He came to England at the invitation of his friend, fellow Trinidadian and cricketer Learie (later Lord) Constantine, and made his name writing on cricket for what was then the *Manchester Guardian*.

When James moved to London, he worked on his history of Haitian independence, *The Black Jacobins*. In 1938, the year his book was published, he moved to the USA, becoming active in Trotskyist politics but never forsaking his interest in philosophy, literature and history. McCarthyism caused his return to London in 1953, and he lived in Willesden and Hampstead before returning to Trinidad, where he was involved in his homeland's struggle for independence, editing *The Nation* newspaper.

For the last 30 years of his life, London was his home, and he enjoyed worldwide fame among the Afro-Caribbean community. Until the 1980s, James travelled more than ever. He was also an honoured guest in Ghana, whose first president, Kwame Nkrumah, had been his protégé. But his welcome ran out when he expressed disillusion when Nkrumah turned to authoritarianism.

Towards the end of his life James was increasingly housebound, but his cramped, two-bedroom flat, above what were then the offices of *Race Today*, became a place of pilgrimage for activists, students, admirers and journalists. The Marxist revolutionary achieved a kind of posthumous establishment blessing when a commemorative blue plaque was unveiled in 2004, during Black History Month.

Address 165 Railton Road, SW9 8BH | Getting there Underground to Brixton (Victoria line) | Hours Viewable from outside only | Tip On the side of the Marks & Spencer supermarket at 446 Brixton Road, London SW9, is a powerful, 30-foot mural of Michelle Obama created by Nottingham-based artist Neequaye Dreph Diane.

24 Cornhill

A door in the Square Mile tells a Brontë story

It is easy to miss but the bottom right panel of the eight in the door at 32 (then 65) Cornhill marks two significant literary events – the visit of Charlotte and Anne Brontë to London in 1848 (the reclusive Emily stayed in Haworth, their home) and their meeting William Makepeace Thackeray (see ch. 96). They did not meet here, so the panel seems to commemorate that all three authors were published by Smith Elder & Co, whose office this was. They met at Thackeray's own house and at the home of the firm's co-founder George Elder. The two sisters came to London because Thomas Newby, who published Emily (*Wuthering Heights*) and Anne (*Agnes Grey*), went on to try to capitalise on the subsequent bestselling success of *Jane Eyre* by marketing Charlotte's *The Tenant of Wildfell Hall* as 'Mr Bell's new novel'.

The Brontë sisters lived most of their lives in the small Yorkshire village of Haworth (although Anne and Charlotte had visited Brussels and both had been governesses) but they travelled to London several times, and attended the opera. Elder had written to 'Acton Bell' (Charlotte's *nom de plume*) to ask why the novel was being offered by another publisher. The confusion was what prompted Charlotte and Anne, out of the blue, to present themselves at the office. Elder was surprised to find that the Brontës were women because convention dictated that they publish under the *noms de plume* (Anne wrote as Currer Bell).

Charlotte regarded Thackeray as a kind of literary hero, to the extent that she had 'respectfully' dedicated *Jane Eyre* to him the previous year. The novel had been the first great success of Smith Elder, who would publish, among others, Mary Gaskell, George Eliot (see ch. 100), Alfred Tennyson and Thomas Hardy. The finely carved door panels were created by Walter Gilbert (1871–1946), who trained in the Arts & Crafts tradition, and worked mainly in metal.

Address 32 Cornhill, EC3V 3SG | **Getting there** Underground to Bank (Northern and Central lines) | **Hours** Always visible | **Tip** Just a five-minute walk away you'll find the foundations of the Temple of Mithras, discovered in 1954 after excavations following the Blitz in 1941; the mystery and intrigue of the cult of the Roman god is caught by the renovation that takes us back to London in 240 A.D. (www.londonmithraeum.com).

Pope's Head Tavern in existence in 1750
belonged to Merchant Taylors Company
The Vintners were prominent in the life of
Cornhill Ward
Thackeray and the Brontes at the publishing
house of Smith Elder & Co. Cowper the poet
Gray the poet Guy the bookseller and founder
of Guys Hospital lived in Cornhill

25 Covent Garden

Johnson meets Boswell, and a great book is born

In 1793, what is now the Balthazar restaurant was the home of the publisher and bookseller Tom Davies. On 16 May he was having tea with his friend, 22-year-old James Boswell, a lawyer and Scottish aristocrat, when Dr Samuel Johnson walked in. The good doctor, as he was known, found great fame when, in 1755, his dictionary was published. It was three years in the writing, for which he was paid 150 guineas and awarded a Crown pension of £300 a year.

Davies, whom Boswell described as 'friendly and hospitable', was once an actor, known for his impersonations of Johnson. He and Johnson were friendly – so much so that when Davies' business fell on hard times, Johnson arranged a benefit for him at Drury Lane, and he was one of the few people whom Johnson allowed to visit during his last illness.

On this occasion, Johnson was displaying (as Boswell later said) 'no passion for clean living' with his strange tics and mannerisms, his 'slovenly' appearance and 'uncouth' speech. Boswell was also apprehensive as he knew of the other man's 'mortal antipathy' toward the Scots. He did not want Davies to mention that he was a Scot, but Davies did. Boswell admitted it and said he could not help it, to which Johnson replied, 'Sir, that I find a very great many of your countrymen cannot help'.

Boswell went on to describe 'the great Mr Johnson' as a 'very big man, [who] is troubled with sore eyes, the palsy and the king's evil [scrofula]'. He made other remarks, flattering and otherwise, about Johnson, but appreciated his humour and knowledge and respected his work. He noted, 'I shall mark what I remember of his conversation'. Indeed he did, and this became his *Life of Johnson*. A landmark in biographical writing, it recorded the subject's words and thoughts in a rounded portrait, in the context of the London they both knew, with its taverns, clubs and meeting places.

Address 4–6 Russell Street, WC2B 5HZ | Getting there Underground to Covent Garden (Piccadilly line) | Hours Viewable outside all hours | Tip Walk south to Savoy Hill to visit the easily overlooked Savoy Chapel. The original was a chapel for a hospital which once stood on the site of the old Savoy Palace. Part of the outside walls goes back to 1502. In 1890 it was the first London church to be electrically lit. It became the chapel of the Royal Victorian Order in 1936 and is the King's private chapel, but is open to the public most days and for Sunday worship (www.royalchapelsavoy.org).

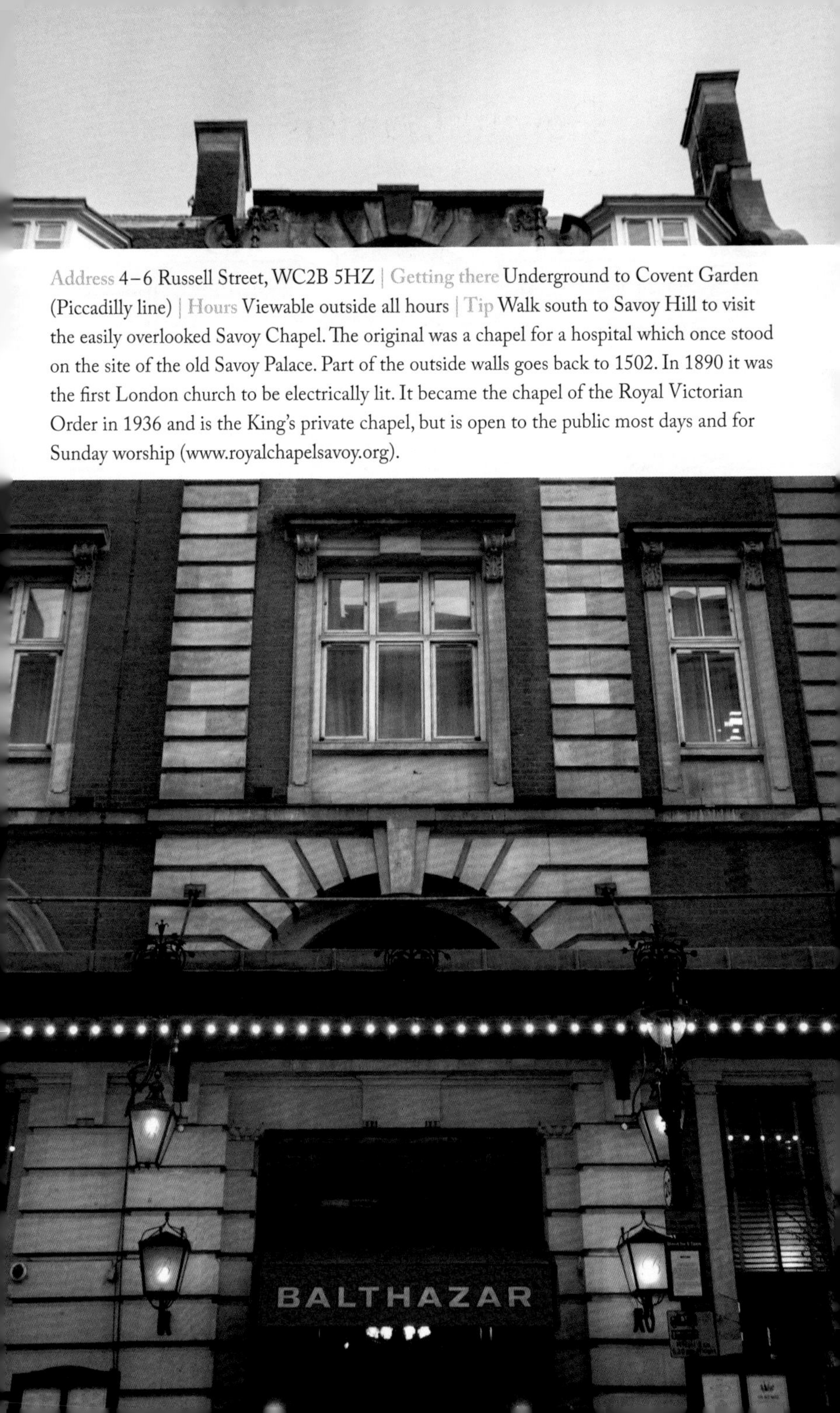

26 Daniel Defoe's Tombstone

A long journey to its present home

How the gravestone of Daniel Defoe went missing from its original location and ended up in a museum over two miles away is a tortuous tale. Defoe lived for 22 years in Stoke Newington, part of the area's nonconformist community. The author of such titles as *Robinson Crusoe*, *Moll Flanders*, and *Journal of the Plague Year*, Defoe died of lethargy – what we now refer to as a stroke – on 24 April, 1731. He passed away at his home in Ropemakers Alley, and was buried in the dissenters' cemetery of Bunhill Fields in the City of London. Defoe produced at least 300 publications, including pamphlets and nine novels, as well as several works of non-fiction.

The last years of Daniel Defoe's life were plagued by financial adversity and the pursuit of creditors. This situation led to property being transferred to his son, and a spiral of mortgaging and re-mortgaging. Despite these efforts, Defoe's debts followed him to the grave – and beyond: one creditor gained administration of the writer's estate two years after his death. In his final year, lodging succeeded lodging in London, as well as a village in Kent. In his last surviving letter, he tells of himself 'sinking under the Weight' of 'Insupportable Sorrows', missing his family, and fearing he would not see his daughter Sophia's child – which, as it transpired, he did not.

In 1870 it was decided that Defoe's tombstone would be replaced by an obelisk. When erected, the ceremony was attended by one of Defoe's great-granddaughters. Samuel Horner, the mason, took the gravestone back to his garden in Bournemouth, and it ended up in a suburb of Southampton in 1885, subsequently being moved to Stoke Newington Library in 1945. The gravestone was again relocated to Hackney Museum, when it opened in 2002, an environment offering improved conditions for conservation. Today it is displayed with a bust of the author.

Address Hackney Museum, 1 Reading Lane, E8 1GQ, +44 (0)208 356 2509, www.hackney-museum@hackney.gov.uk | Getting there Overground to Dalston Kingsland or Underground to Bethnal Green (Central line) and then bus 106 or 254 to Hackney Town Hall | Hours Tue, Wed & Fri 9.30am–5.30pm, Thu 9.30am–8pm, Sat 10am–5pm | Tip Head north for Ridley Road market. Opened in 1920, it's famous for its range of traditional and exotic foods, often sold from traditional barrows, reflecting the area's multicultural population. The market featured in the eponymous novel and resultant TV series about its association with post-war fascism.

27 Dean Street

Marx's love life above a London restaurant

In a brief memoir, Jenny, wife of Karl Marx (see ch. 53), wrote that 'an event occurred which I do not wish to relate here in detail, although it contributed to an increase in our worries, both personal and others'. That event, which took place in June 1851, in what Marx called 'an old hovel – two evil, frightful rooms', was the birth of Henry Frederick Demuth. The mother, Helen Demuth, was the Marxes' faithful servant and companion for four decades. But who was the father? The birth certificate has no name, but Jenny, who had herself given birth to the couple's fourth child some months earlier, went into a hysterical collapse at Freddy's birth. Frederick Engels, Marx's wealthy collaborator and patron, allowed himself to be regarded as the father. But on his death bed he confessed the truth to Marx's youngest child, Eleanor, who wept bitterly. She later became close to her half-brother, until her suicide in 1898, aged 43.

The Marxes lived at 28 Dean Street from 1850 to 1856 (the blue plaque mistakenly says 1851). Marx came to England from Germany in 1845, with Engels, and returned to live permanently with his family in 1849 after being expelled from his native country. He moved to this address only two years after he and Engels had published *The Communist Manifesto*. From Dean Street, Marx would walk to the British Museum reading room, where he wrote most of *Das Kapital*. His fortunes were at a low ebb: he fought off creditors, his hopes for revolution in Europe had been dashed, tensions with his wife were fraught even before the birth, and two of the Marxes' then five children died.

Freddy was fostered by a couple named Lewis in Hackney soon after birth. He later became a socialist activist, becoming a founder of the Hackney Labour Party. Jenny died in 1881, Marx in 1883, and Helen in 1890. It is now widely accepted by historians that the father of Communism was also the father of an illegitimate child.

Address Quo Vadis Restaurant, 22-26 Dean Street, W1D 3LL, +44 (0)207 437 9585, www.quovadissoho.co.uk | Getting there Underground to Tottenham Court Road (Central, Elizabeth and Northern lines) or Leicester Square (Northern and Piccadilly lines) | Hours Daily 12.30–2.30pm, 5.30–10pm | Tip There has been a Chinese community in London since the 19th century, and in the 1950s, as their numbers grew, they moved from the East End to Soho. Chinese restaurants and shops selling Chinese medicines and goods proliferate in the area, which is also the venue for the annual Chinese New Year festival.

28 Down House

Where Darwin explained our origins

Few places could be as different as the Galapagos Islands in the eastern Pacific and Down House in the rural outer reaches of London. But after spending five weeks on the islands in 1835, during his voyage on HMS *Beagle*, Charles Darwin returned to his home in Downe to consider his observations of the wildlife he had seen, to formulate his theory of evolution. It was in the ground floor study of the house that he wrote *On the Origin of Species by Means of Natural Selection*. Published in 1859, this proved to be one of the most influential books ever to appear in print.

Darwin lived in the Grade I-listed house for 40 years until his death in 1882. He and his wife Emma took possession in 1842, along with their two children, William and Anne. Nine days after the Darwins moved to the house, Etty, their third child, was born, and over the next 14 years another six children were born at Down. They were occasionally permitted to enter the study, on the understanding that they did not disturb their father.

Apart from a wish by the Darwins to get away from the noise of London, where they lived on Gower Street (see ch. 33), they were attracted to the countryside. Of the house, Darwin wrote, 'being situated on rather high table-land, [it] has somewhat of a desolate air ... The charm of the place to me is that almost every field is intersected (as alas is our's) by one or more foot-paths – I never saw so many walks in any other country.' The couple remodelled the house and its extensive gardens. The gardens were for more than leisure, but an open-air laboratory. Visitors can still see this today, and can walk Darwin's 'thinking path', passing bountiful vegetable patches and fragrant flower beds. Emma died at the house in 1896, and it later became a girls' school where, during the First World War, one pupil was the future novelist, Elizabeth Bowen (see ch. 38).

Address Luxted Road, Downe, Kent, BR6 7JT, +44 (0)370 333 1181, www.english-heritage.org.uk | Getting there Trains to Chelsfield or Orpington, R8 bus which passes the house, or 146 bus to Downe village | Hours Daily 10am–5pm | Tip Six miles from Down is Quebec House, 18th-century childhood home of General James Wolfe, victor in the Battle of Quebec (1759), where he also died.

29 Dr Dee's Library

The 'lost' library in an unusual place

The Royal College of Physicians is the oldest medical college in the UK, but perhaps not the obvious venue for a collection of antiquarian books. The college has been collecting since its foundation in 1518, and includes a first edition of Chaucer's *The Canterbury Tales*, and medical texts by Greek, Roman and Arab doctors.

However, perhaps the most usual and rarest part of the collection in the library is that of Doctor John Dee. Born only nine years after the college's foundation, he was one of Tudor England's most extraordinary figures – a polymath, with interests in almost all branches of learning. He was also an Elizabethan courtier (he was a astronomer to Elizabeth I), an adviser on several navigations of the New World, and also made many journeys to the Continent.

His creation and loss of one of the greatest private libraries of his time may be his most enduring achievement. He claimed to own 3,000 books and 1,000 manuscripts housed in his Thames-side home, far more than in the libraries of Oxford and Cambridge universities. They reflected his catholic interests: among them, natural history, music, astronomy, astrology, military history, mathematics, cryptography, ancient history, alchemy, and the world of angels. His scholarship was such that his many annotations, in elegant italic, have themselves been subject to academic study.

There are two accounts of how so much of Dee's library was lost. He said that his brother-in-law, to whom he entrusted it while he went to Europe, 'unduly sold it presently on my departure'. But it is also claimed that books were stolen by aggrieved former associates. He recovered only some of the collection. Much of what was unrecovered passed to other hands. Fortunately, much came to the Marquis of Dorchester, for on his death in 1680 (Dee had died 71 years before) it passed to the RCP, which has the largest holding of his printed books.

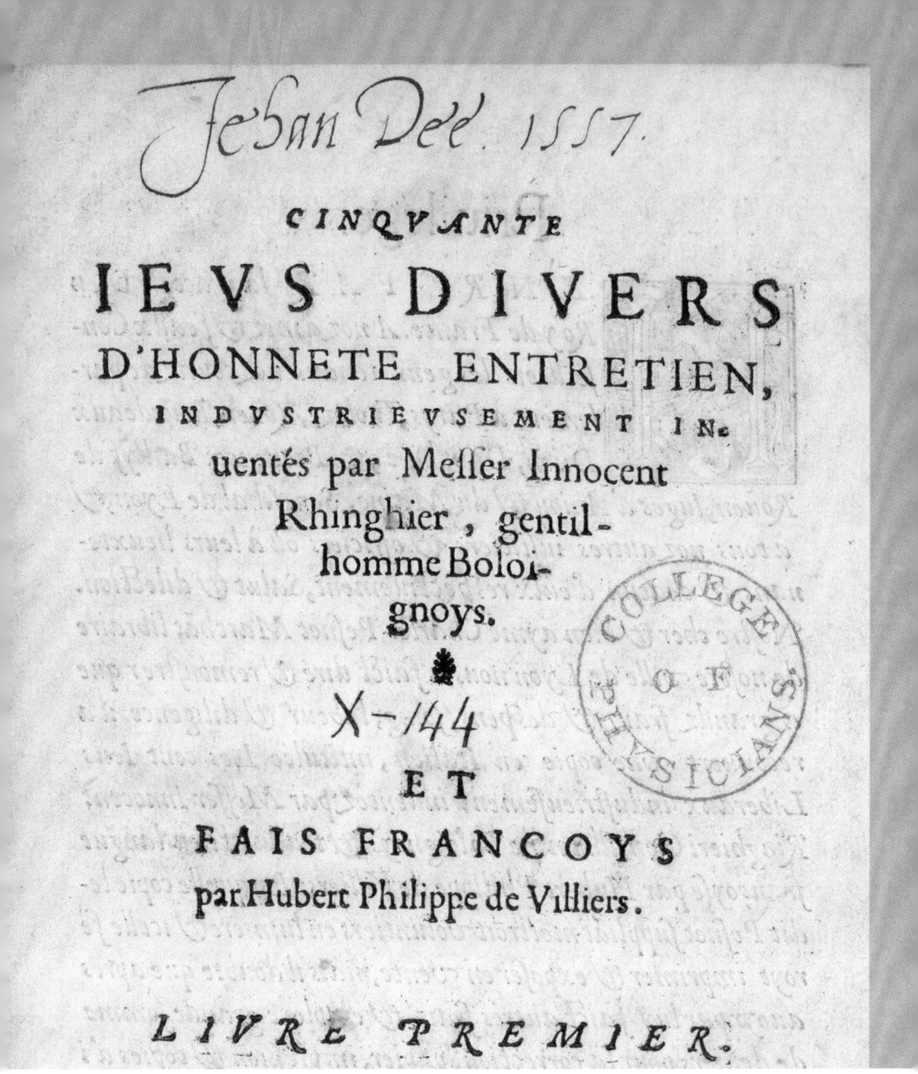

Jehan Dee. 1557.

CINQVANTE

IEVS DIVERS

D'HONNETE ENTRETIEN,

INDVSTRIEVSEMENT IN-
uentés par Meſſer Innocent
Rhinghier, gentil-
homme Boloi-
gnoys.

ET

FAIS FRANCOYS

par Hubert Philippe de Villiers.

LIVRE PREMIER.

Address Royal College of Physicians, 11 St Andrews Place, Regent's Park, NW1 4LE, +44 (0)203 075 1313, www.rcplondon.ac.uk | Getting there Underground to Regent's Park (Bakerloo line) or Great Portland Street (Metropolitan, Circle and Hammersmith & City lines) | Hours Tue–Thu 9.30am–4.30pm; appointments on +44 (0)203 075 1313 and via history@rcplondon.ac.uk | Tip Harley Street is a synonym for (private) medical practice and is itself an 18th- century street of handsome houses in varied design. There are few private houses here now. Doctors came in the mid-19th century and William Gladstone lived at No. 73.

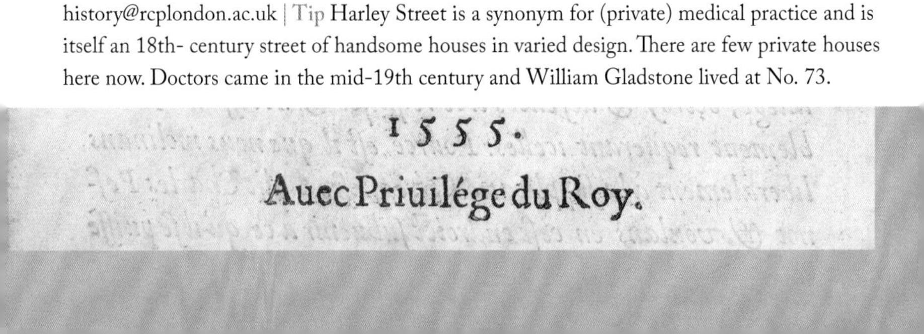

1555.

Auec Priuilége du Roy.

30 Farm Street Church

Brideshead had its origins here

How better to advertise one of the most important events in your life than to invite a renowned gossip columnist as your only guest? In 1928, Evelyn Waugh became very famous when his first novel, *Decline and Fall,* was published. In September 1930, he was received into the Catholic Church in this strikingly beautiful, sumptuous Gothic Revival Jesuit Church of the Immaculate Conception. There was one problem – Waugh was married to a wife who had deserted him in the first months of marriage.

The marriage was annulled by the Church, and he remarried four years later. Waugh, who would become one of the most public of Catholics, invited as his witness his friend, the journalist, writer and future Labour MP – and Soviet agent – Tom Driberg, who was then the diarist William Hickey of the *Daily Express.* The reprobate High Anglican was puzzled and flattered. It seems likely that Waugh calculated that paragraphs in a national newspaper would obviate him the chore of having to write letters of explanation to friends.

The year before, Waugh had written to his brother, Alec: 'The trouble about the world today is that there's not enough religion in it. There's nothing to stop young people doing whatever they feel like doing at the moment'. The Church was giving Waugh answers he was unable to find elsewhere. To him, the world was 'unintelligible and unendurable without God'. For him, the Catholic Church was revered because it was true and universal, and 'Christianity exists in its most complete and vital form in the Roman Catholic Church'.

Such deceptive simplicity bespoke a matter-of-factness about belief once accepted. A rather different form of matter-of-factness was that after the event, Waugh and Driberg joined friends for dinner at the Café Royal. Without Waugh's conversion, we would have been denied one of his greatest novels: *Brideshead Revisited.*

Address Church of the Immaculate Conception, 114 Mount Street, W1K 3AH, +44 (0)207 529 4829, www.farmstreet.org.uk | Getting there Underground to Green Park (Victoria, Jubilee, and Piccadilly lines) | Hours See website for current information and mass times | Tip Royal Opera Arcade was London's first shopping arcade, designed by John Nash. Its upmarket shops sell everything you could want for shooting and fishing.

31 Flemings Hotel

Miss Marple's London holiday

Flemings Hotel is the location for *At Bertram's Hotel*, published in 1965, the penultimate novel featuring Agatha Christie's amateur detective, Miss Marple. Like many of Christie's novels, it's set in a closed environment. The novel, published in magazines prior to appearing in book form, gives the hotel a life of its own, a community of assorted types. The characters are very much the Christie kind: in this case a clergyman, an aristocratic woman, a colonel, a general, a beautiful young heiress, a racing driver, and a duke!

The hotel was restored to its original condition: 'By 1955 it looked precisely as it had looked in 1939 – dignified, unostentatious, and quietly expensive,' wrote Christie. It has 'a big central lounge ... two magnificent coal fires; besides them big coal scuttles shone in the way they used to shine when Edwardian housemaids polished them ... A general appearance of rich red velvet and plushy cosiness.' Christie's notes refer to the kind of hotel she wanted to create: 'Real bit of old England ... Edwardian hotel ... "Only get muffins at Bertram's".' It was in a 'pocket' of London.

Miss Marple forsakes rural life in her cottage, 'Danemead' in St Mary Mead, to stay for two weeks at the hotel, which she visited when young, after her nephew treats her. She finds the hotel both a refuge from the life of the capital, whilst also enjoying its attractions (she visits the Army & Navy store, once in Victoria Street, Westminster, as had the young Christie) – and she solves a murder. In order to disguise Flemings, Christie discussed with her agent how she would change the hotel's name and that of the street where it was situated, as well as the name of the manager from his Italian name to a pseudonym. These clues belie the common mistake (repeated by some biographers) that it is nearby Brown's Hotel. The novel sold 50,000 copies within the first month of publication.

Address Half Moon Street, W1J 7BH, +44 (0)207 499 0000, www.flemings-mayfair.co.uk | Getting there Underground to Green Park (Piccadilly, Victoria lines and Jubilee lines) | Hours 24 hours | Tip The Royal Academy for permanent and special art exhibitions is just around the corner in Piccadilly (www.royalacademy.org.uk).

32 Freud Meets Dalí

Meeting of an unlikely couple

By June 1938 Sigmund Freud was world-famous through books such as *The Interpretation of Dreams* and *The Psychopathology of Everyday Life*. Born in 1856 in Freiberg, now part of the Czech Republic, he arrived in Britain in 1938, with his wife Martha and youngest daughter, Anna, refugees from the Nazis after their annexation of Austria.

On 19 July, then temporarily living at 39 Elsworthy, Freud received a visitor. Only 34, Salvador Dalí was already a widely recognised Surrealist painter. Freud had little time for such avant-garde movements, but as a student in Madrid, Dalí had read Freud's work, and eagerly studied his ideas on dreams, sexuality and the unconscious. In his autobiography, Dalí recounts having 'long and exhaustive imaginary conversations' with Freud, and of *Dreams*, he said, 'I was seized with a real vice of self-interpretation, not only of my dreams but of everything that happened to me'. The artist was anxious to be considered intellectually and artistically serious by Freud. Dalí brought with him his *The Metamorphosis of Narcissus*, hoping to engage Freud in a psychoanalytic discussion of narcissism.

Dalí made a significant impression, 'I have never seen a more complete example of a Spaniard. What a fanatic!' Freud told the writer Stefan Zweig, who introduced the two men. Freud also commented that 'In classic paintings I look for the unconscious, but in your paintings I look for the conscious'. Dalí took this as criticism, but while Freud said that he had seen the Surrealists as 'absolute cranks', he found that Dalí 'with his candid and fanatical eyes, and his undeniable technical mastery, has made me reconsider my opinion'.

In September 1939, a year after moving to Maresfield Gardens (now the Freud Museum) 81-year-old Freud died. Dalí's sketch of Freud was bequeathed to the museum by a wealthy American woman in 1989 and can be seen there today.

Address 39 Elsworthy Road, NW3 3DL; Freud Museum, 20 Maresfield Gardens, NW3 5SX, +44 (0)207 435 2002, www.freud.org.uk | Getting there Elsworthy Road Overground to South Hampstead; Freud Museum Underground to Finchley Road (Metropolitan and District lines), Hampstead (Northern line), and Overground to Finchley Road & Frognal | Hours Elsworthy Road, outside viewing only; Freud Museum, Wed–Sun 10.30am–5pm | Tip Fenton House, a 17th century merchant's residence, is nearby. It has a collection of decorative porcelain, Georgian furniture and 17th century needlework, early keyboard instruments, and a walled garden with orchard, rose gardens, terraces and lawns.

33 Gower Street

Ottoline Morrell entertains the literati

Ottoline Morrell was an aristocrat, related to the Duke of Wellington and the Royal family. Her salon started in 1907, when she and her pacifist husband, Liberal MP Philip Morrell, whose beliefs she shared, lived at 44 Bedford Square. When they sold the large house in 1927, it was a shock to move to a more modest home, but it was here that Morrell spent the last 10 years of her life. Financial difficulties caused them to sell their country home, Garsington Manor, near Oxford, that same year.

Ottoline Morrell was a great hostess. On Thursdays, their home at No 10 was visited by such luminaries as T.S. Eliot (see ch. 76), Maynard Keynes, Bertrand Russell – one of Morrell's many lovers, as she and her husband enjoyed an open marriage – W.B. Yeats (see ch. 106), Julian and Aldous Huxley, and the composer Dame Ethel Smyth. Morrell was also patron to artists such as Stanley Spencer, Mark Gertler and Dora Carrington. Some people loved her, and she amused others, but there were those, such as Virginia Woolf, Vanessa Bell, and Lytton Strachey, who sniggered at her mannerisms, voice, beliefs, and distinctive appearance: Ottoline Morrell was very tall, with what might be described as a 'horse-like' face, and wore striking clothes.

For a woman who produced no great work herself, she is well remembered in literary and artistic circles. There are portraits of her by Cecil Beaton, Henry Lamb, Duncan Grant, and Augustus John, and she is even depicted in films. In novels, she is portrayed unpleasantly as Mrs Bidlake in Aldous Huxley's *Point Counter Point*, cruelly as Hermione Roddice in D. H. Lawrence's *Women in Love* (see ch. 72), and sympathetically as Lady Caroline Bury in Graham Greene's *It's A Battlefield.* Few people passing 10 Gower Street today would guess at the passions – both artistic and sexual – laughter, conversations, and guests, that once filled this house.

Address 10 Gower Street, WC1E 6HE | Getting there Underground to Tottenham Court Road (Central, Elizabeth and Northern lines) | Hours Always visible | Tip Just off Gower Street is the Petrie Museum, home to one of the world's greatest collections of Egyptian and Sudanese archaeology (www.ucl.ac.uk/culture/petrie-museum).

34 Great Russell Street

A place of contrasting styles and stylists

In 1913, Harold Munro, founder and editor of the influential *Poetry Review*, founded the Poetry Bookshop at 35 Devonshire (now Boswell) Street, Bloomsbury. When the lease expired in 1926, aided by a loan from his mother, he moved the bookshop to Great Russell Street (now Munchkins café), diagonally across the street from the British Museum. Munro commissioned American Art Deco poster artist Edward McKnight Kauffer to produce a bright shop sign showing an illustrated book and a lyre. However, this did not find favour with the landlord, the Duke of Bedford, who ordered that it be repainted white.

T. S. Eliot (see ch. 76) opened the bookshop at a formal ceremony, for which 600 invitations were issued. The shop was a focus for the contrasting styles of the Imagists and the Georgians. There were musical as well as poetry recitals, and the first London performance of Igor Stravinsky's Rites of Spring took place at its original premises.

The bookshop attracted many leading literary figures of the day, including the poets Wilfred Owen and the American Robert Frost. Frost lived in the bookshop for a while, as did the First World War poet Wilfred Wilson Gibson. In fact, Gibson met Frost in Devonshire Street, where Frost was also to meet the novelist and poet Robert Graves, who was then a soldier. When Frost first turned up, Munro claimed to know he was an American by his shoes!

Munro's evangelism for poetry allowed him to attract performers as different as Walter de la Mare and Ezra Pound. But the bookshop also sold and published work by living poets such as Richard Aldington and Charlotte Mew. The atmosphere of Devonshire Street did not wholly transfer to Great Russell Street, however. Thomas and Owen died in the trenches, and Frost left for the United States. When Munro died of tuberculosis in 1932, the shop struggled on until its eventual closure three years later.

Address 38 Great Russell Street, WC2 3PP, +44 (0)207 636 2775 | Getting there Underground to Tottenham Court Road (Elizabeth, Northern and Central lines), or Goodge Street (Northern line) | Hours Daily 9am–10pm | Tip Visit the British Museum across the street to see the Rosetta Stone, discovered in Rashid (Rosetta) in Egypt; 15 years of deciphering revealed this to be the key to Egyptian hieroglyphs.

35_ Grey Court

Cardinal Newman's happy childhood

Ham is now pleasantly situated on the western outskirts of London, but when John Henry Newman's parents bought Grey Court (now Newman House) before he was born in 1801, it was deep in the English countryside. The Newmans had a London home in Bloomsbury, but it is perhaps appropriate that Grey Court is now part of the school from which it takes its name, for here Newman was happiest. This was so much so that he wrote: 'When, at school, I dreamed of heaven, the scene was Ham.' When he was 60, he said that he knew more about Grey Court 'than any house I have been in since, and could pass examinations on it'.

When the family placed candles in their windows to mark the country's victory at the Battle of Trafalgar, this may have inspired his hymn *Lead, kindly light,* written in 1833 when he was a young Anglican clergyman. But in 1864 he published *Apologia Pro Vita Sua*, his spiritual autobiography. This was a defence of his decision to resign from the Church of England in 1844, a prelude to his reception into the Catholic Church two years later. Created a cardinal in 1879, he had long been a major influential figure in British religious life: a leading figure, first in the Church of England's Anglo-Catholic Oxford Movement, and then, in his new home, as a Catholic in the 19th century as a counterweight to the strong anti-Catholicism sentiment of his time. The book remains in print and is a spirited defence of the Church.

Newman was unusual, among clergy, in being both author and poet – his long prose poem, *The Dream of Gerontius*, was set to music by Edward Elgar. His *Grammar of Assent* makes the case for religious belief. His *Idea of the University* is credited with the British belief that higher education should produce generalists, not narrow specialists, and that non-vocational subjects can train the mind. Newman himself founded what is now University College, Dublin.

Address Ham Street, TW10 7HN | **Getting there** Train to Richmond, then bus 317 to Ham Street | **Hours** Viewable from outside only | **Tip** Less than a 15-minute walk away, Ham House and Garden is a striking 17th century Stuart House, with a unique collection of cabinets and artwork. The cherry garden is delightful, with original 17th century statues of Bacchus (www.nationaltrust.org.uk).

36 Guildhall

Home of the Booker prize

The Guildhall is forever associated with the annual ceremony of the Booker Prize, because, since at least the 1980s, with only a few exceptions, the glittering prize was matched by this glittering location: the Great Hall, built in 1411, and seat of the City of London Corporation since the Middle Ages. The last time the Booker presentation took place here was in 2019.

The prize was founded in 1969 as the Booker Prize for Fiction (known as the Mann Booker Prize from 2002 to 2019) for writers who were citizens of the UK, Ireland, the Commonwealth, South Africa, and later Zimbabwe. In 2013, the entry criterion was extended to any novel published anywhere in the world in English and published in the UK or Ireland. It has become one of the world's richest literary awards. In 1970 Bernice Rubens became the first female winner. In 2013 Eleanor Catton became the youngest winner with *The Luminaries*. Hilary Mantel (see ch. 97) is the only female author to win the prize more than once, with the first two parts of her Cromwell trilogy, *Wolf Hall* (2009) and *Bring Up the Bodies* (2012). The first American winner under the new rules was Paul Beatty with his novel *The Sellout*, in 2016.

Before the Booker, book awards had less public impact. A winner might sell another 500 to 1,000 copies, whereas in France, the Goncourt might attract an extra 500,000. That the prize would enhance reading was shown with the first award in 1969 with P. J. Newby's *Something to Answer For*, given at a drinks reception at the Stationer's Hall (see ch. 83). It appeared in the *Evening Standard*'s bestseller list, the first time that a British novel had made an entry on such a list as a result of winning an award. The prize boosted authors, booksellers and publishers, but it was really after being televised in 1981 that it ignited an interest in modern English-language literary fiction.

Address 71 Basinghall Street, EC2 7HH, +44 (0)207 606 3030, www.guildhall.cityoflondon.gov.uk | **Getting there** Underground to Moorgate (District, Circle and Metropolitan lines) or Overground or Underground to Cannon Street (District and Circle lines) | **Hours** See website for current information on visiting | **Tip** Richard Rogers' Lloyd's of London building at 1 Lime Street was built in 1983, although the origins of Lloyd's stretch to the coffee houses of the late 17th century. With its external stainless steel piping, this building reflects the design language of the Pompidou Centre in Paris, which had the same architect.

37 Hazlitt's

Where William's 'happy' life came to an end

In what is now a hotel bearing his name, William Hazlitt, essayist, novelist, drama critic and philosopher, lived in a small room at the back of the house. He died there in 1830, aged 52. Born in Kent, he moved to London in his teens intending to become a painter, like his elder brother, John. But in 1812 he took up journalism, contributing to the *Morning Chronicle* and *The Examiner*, and lecturing. *The Round Table*, his first collection of essays (1817), was followed four years later by *Table-Talk*. His greatest literary success was *Spirit of the Age or, Contemporary Portraits*, in which he wrote about Lord Byron, Jeremy Bentham (see ch. 101) and other contemporaries. The third and fourth volumes of his life of Napoleon appeared posthumously.

Having been arrested for debt, Hazlitt was stalked by poverty when he moved to the apartment in this four-storey Georgian house. Despite ill health, he wrote for *The London Weekly Review* and *The Court Journal*. More frequent bouts of illness caused him to retreat within himself, yet he still wrote some notable essays, mainly for *The New Monthly Magazine*. For *The Atlas* he wrote an essay appropriately entitled 'The sick chamber'.

Between two unsuccessful marriages, Hazlitt became obsessed with the daughter of his landlord elsewhere in London. She was 22 years his senior, and played fast and loose with Hazlitt and another lodger, with whom she eventually departed. Hazlitt's circle included Charles and Mary Lamb, Samuel Taylor Coleridge, and William Wordsworth, but his health declined to the extent that he could not even receive friends. Eventually, he was confined to bed, cared for by his son, William, who, along with Charles Lamb, was with him at his death. His funeral was attended by very few people, but his last words are said to have been, 'Well, I've had a happy life'. The writer's grave can be seen in nearby St Anne's churchyard.

Address 6 Frith Street, W1D 3JA, +44 (0)20 7434 1771, www.hazlittshotel.com | **Getting there** Underground to Tottenham Court Road (Central, Elizabeth and Northern lines) or Leicester Square (Northern and Piccadilly lines) | **Hours** Open 24 hours | **Tip** Ronnie Scott's Club is one of the most famous music venues in the country. Excelling in jazz, the constantly changing programme offers something for every jazz lover (www.ronniescotts.co.uk).

38 Henrietta Street

Rallying cry for the Left

Victor Gollancz started his eponymous publishing company in 1927 at 14 Henrietta Street in Covent Garden, and would go on to acquire authors such as Daphne du Maurier, Elizabeth Bowen and Kingsley Amis. In May 1936 he founded the Left Book Club, a subscription service, 'to help in the terribly urgent struggle for world peace and against fascism'. The enterprise, established with the help Sir Stafford Cripps and John Strachey, two future Labour Cabinet ministers, was something of a movement: not only was there a broadly shared political outlook among members, but there were also 1,500 discussion groups allied around the books, and an annual rally. Subscribers were offered a book each month, and also received a newsletter, which engaged in discussion rather than simply being an advertising vehicle.

The books had distinctive coloured covers: orange for paperbacks, red for hardbacks. Authors included the Communist-leaning cleric Hewlett Johnson (with whom Gollancz fell out over the Nazi-Soviet Pact), Strachey and Cripps, the future prime minister Clement Attlee, poet Stephen Spender, and the writers Arthur Koestler and George Orwell, whose *The Road to Wigan Pier* was published with amendments: Gollancz was a very interventionist editor.

Membership reached 20,000 in the first year, and the following year peaked at 57,000. Numbers decreased, however, as Communists left when the club came out against the Nazi-Soviet Pact in 1939. Wartime paper rationing did nothing to help matters, and Gollancz published his last book in 1948. By that time the club had a big achievement under its belt, however: it is largely credited with the leftward political swing in the country that brought Labour to power in 1945.

When Gollancz suffered a stroke in 1966 his daughter Livia, an accomplished professional musician, ran the company until 1989, when it was sold to Houghton Mifflin.

Address 14 Henrietta Street, WC2E 8QG | Getting there Underground to Covent Garden (Piccadilly line) | Hours Viewable from outside 24 hours | Tip Charing Cross, five minutes' walk away, is where Edward I erected a cross at the 12 resting places from Lincoln to Westminster for the funeral of Queen Eleanor of Castile in 1290. All mileage distances throughout Britain are measured from here.

39 Heywood Hill Bookshop

A novelist who sold other people's books

Nancy Mitford, the eldest of six sisters, had already published four novels when she came to work in this shop in March 1942. At the time she was recovering from an ectopic pregnancy following a failed love affair with a Free French officer during World War II, which ended her marriage. Her sociable character and witty repartee helped establish Heywood Hill's shop as a centre of London social and literary life during the 1940s.

She earned £3 a week, and often walked for around an hour to and from her home in Maida Vale to save the bus fare. According to her sister, Deborah, Duchess of Devonshire, one evening she forgot to lock up and arrived the next day to find the shop 'full of wandering people trying to buy books from each other'. Nancy's charm, wit and gregariousness made the shop popular, and its customers numbered her great friend Evelyn Waugh (see ch. 30), Anthony Powell and Osbert Sitwell. Her attributes were all the more necessary when the owner, Heywood Hill, was called up late in 1942, and his wife, Anne, left to have her first baby, leaving Nancy in the role of manager.

Mitford had lost interest in writing when her novel *Pigeon Pie* was unsuccessful when it appeared in 1940, but, with Waugh's encouragement, she published *The Pursuit of Love* in 1945. The bookshop gave her three months' leave to write her novel – she never returned.

The book was a romantic comedy with autobiographical elements, with friends and family appearing in disguise. It sold 200,000 copies within a year of publication, and established Mitford as a best-seller. It was, her biographer says, 'the perfect antidote to the long war years of hardship and austerity, providing the undernourished public with its favourite ingredients: love, childhood and the English upper classes.' *The Pursuit of Love* and *Love In a Cold Climate*, published in 1949, have enchanted readers ever since.

Address 10 Curzon Street, W1 5HH, +44 (0)20 7629 0647, www.heywoodhill.com | **Getting there** Underground to Green Park (Piccadilly, Jubilee, and Victoria lines) | **Hours** Mon–Fri 9.30am–6pm | **Tip** At the Hyde Park end of Piccadilly is Apsley House, or No. 1, London, as it was known when the Duke of Wellington lived here. A beautiful Georgian building whose interiors literally glitter, it has a superb art collection.

40_Highgate Cemetery

Muse exhumed for poems from the grave

Elizabeth Siddal was an acclaimed beauty, taken up as a model in the early years of the Pre-Raphaelite Brotherhood. She became a painter in that tradition, and also a poet. The poet and painter Dante Gabriel Rossetti, whom she would marry in 1860, was largely responsible for Siddal's artistic image: his studies of her in pen and pencil, usually reading or sleeping, show an uneducated, ordinary girl – she was a milliner and dressmaker of working class origins – with a fragile, idealised beauty. As one writer says, he showed 'the pathos of her strange beauty… in heavy lids drooping over agate-coloured eyes, wings of copper-red hair framing a face singular in its remoteness'. Even in death, her beauty was, reputedly, undiminished.

When Lizzie, as she was known, committed suicide in 1862, she was buried in Highgate, and Rossetti placed a manuscript of his new poems between her hair and cheek. Years later, however, by this time famous, a heavy drinker and addicted to chloral, he found himself in need of money. As a solution, Rossetti's unscrupulous agent Charles Augustus Howell prevailed on him to have the grave opened, retrieve the poems and publish them.

Permission was sought from the Home Secretary, but Frances Rossetti, his mother and the owner of the grave, which contained other members of her family, was excluded from the decision. Rossetti's guilt did not allow him to attend, so it was Howell who, with only a lawyer present, dug the grave late at night, illuminated by just a fire. Howell declared not only that the body was perfectly preserved, but also that Lizzie's still copper-coloured hair had continued to grow, now filled the coffin and had to be disentangled from the pages. The poems were published in 1870. Howell's likely over-active imagination has fed into the myth of the Pre-Raphaelites and Lizzie, as the eternal and uncorrupted hereafter.

AH DIO AJUTAMI TU
ALSO OF
FRANCES MARY LAVINIA.
BELOVED WIFE OF THE ABOVE NAMED
GABRIELE ROSSETTI.
BORN APRIL 27TH 1800. DIED APRIL 8TH 1886.
ALSO OF
WILLIAM MICHAEL ROSSETTI.
SON OF THE ABOVE.
BORN 25TH SEPTEMBER 1829.
DIED 5TH FEBRUARY 1919.
HAVING SEEN THE REALISATION OF ITALIAN UNITY

Address Swains Lane, N6 6PJ, +44 (0)28 340 1834, www.highgatecemetery.org | **Getting there** Underground to Archway (Northern line) | **Hours** Daily 10am–4pm; self-conducted tour £10; guided tour £15 | **Tip** On the other side of Waterlow Park, near the cemetery, is a statue of a black cat on Highgate Hill. This is said to be where a forlorn Dick Whittington and his pet stopped, when he heard the sound of Bow Bells (very unlikely!) calling him to return, declaring his destiny as three times Lord Mayor of London.

41 Holland House

A place for literature, politics and good talk

The grandeur of the complete east wing and the damaged west one stand either side of the central cloister or south façade. This itself is divided by the grand entrance, and is all that remains of this early Jacobean country house following war-time bombing, and part-demolition in the 1950s. Once the centre of Whig politics and scene of many literary parties, the house is set in a 500-acre estate, some of which is now Holland Park. It was built by an aristocratic family in 1605, and was visited by members of the royal family, including King James I. When it was an army headquarters, Oliver Cromwell visited, too.

For three years until his death in 1719, it was the home of the writer Joseph Addison, founder of *The Spectator*. Later, the great Whig Charles James Fox, who grew up here as the son of the first Baron Holland, created a social and political circle. When he died in 1806, his nephew, Henry Vassall-Fox, the third baron, inherited the property. Wishing to keep alive his uncle's memory and influence, he continued the tradition, along with his wife, Elizabeth. It became known as the Holland House Set, and lasted from 1797 to 1845.

It was at one such gathering in 1812 that the poet Lord Byron met his future lover, Lady Caroline Lamb, whose husband, Lord Melbourne, became the Whig prime minister after her death. She satirised the set in her novel *Glenavon*, while Byron's notoriously rakish behaviour was such that she famously dubbed him 'mad, bad and dangerous to know'. In later years the historian Thomas Babington Macaulay, the novelists Charles Dickens (see ch. 19) and Walter Scott, and the novelist and future prime minister Benjamin Disraeli (see ch. 82), were guests. Today, young people can imbibe the glories of the past, as part of the house is now a youth hostel, while the elegant glass and stone Orangery is now a wedding venue.

Address Ilchester Place, W8 6LU | Getting there Underground to High Street Kensington (Circle and District lines) | Hours Daily 7.30am until 30 minutes before dusk | Tip Behind the house, in 22-acre Holland Park, is the peaceful Kyoto Garden. Opened in 1991 as a gift from the city of Kyoto to commemorate friendship between Japan and Great Britain, it has waterfalls, a pond and stone bridges.

42 Imperial War Museum

Antonia White sees through glass

In November 1922, 23-year-old Antonia White was accompanied by her father under the portico of Wren's Bethlem Hospital – now the Imperial War Museum. She was suffering from 'maniacal excitement', incoherent and hyperactive, and said to be a danger to herself and others. There, she was certified as insane. Forcibly fed and heavily sedated during much of her 10-month stay, she was kept in a cell. She described this as 'dirty distemper on the walls, and something like a large manger to sleep in with thick cotton sheets'. Her breakdown was partly occasioned by the annulment of her marriage to Reginald Henry (Reggie) Green-Wilkinson, on the grounds of non-consummation.

She referred to her illness, involving severe hallucinations, as 'the beast'. Yet even when 'in the power of the beast', she was detached and could observe herself. She regarded her illness, distressing as it was, as giving another dimension to life, and helping to make her a writer. When admitted, White was known, if at all, for stories in newspapers. In 1933, she published *Frost in May*, the first of a quartet of slim autobiographical novels, taking her alter ego from the ages of 9 to 23. Severely affected by writer's block, the fruit of White's incarceration, *Beyond the Glass* – the most technically ambitious of her novels – did not appear until 1954. After her four novels, she wrote only short stories, and two books on cats. The Imperial War Museum took over the building in 1930 and she visited the cell in which she had been confined in 1936; a short story – 'Surprise Visit' – was the result.

White died in 1980, aged 81, after a life dogged by mental instability. When her father converted to Catholicism, she was also received into the Church as a child. At the time of her death, she was reconciled to the Church, but not to one of the two daughters who resulted from two further marriages.

Address Lambeth Road, SE1 6HZ, +44 (0)207 416 5000, www.iwm.org.uk | Getting there Underground to Lambeth North (Bakerloo line) | Hours Daily 10am–6pm | Tip Two stops on the Underground from Elephant & Castle to London Bridge will take you within a 5-minute walk of the beribboned, locked metal gates of Cross Bones Graveyard on Redcross Way. Until the 17th century, prostitutes were buried here. Later a Christian cemetery for the poor, it was closed in 1852 following an estimated 15,000 burials.

43 Islington History Centre

The playwright who defaced books

There are several ways to ensure your local library has the books you want – order them, reserve online or email the librarian, for example. But when, in the early 1960s, playwright Joe Orton and his lover Kenneth Halliwell were unimpressed by the choice on the shelves in their local libraries in Islington, they adopted an unusual approach: defacing books. Collages of cut-outs of monkeys, tattooed torsos, and surreal images, homoerotic or sexually provocative, culled from magazines and newspaper colour supplements, adorned the books. Scandalous texts were sometimes added, or titles rewritten: for example, Emlyn Williams' *Night Must Fall* became *Knickers Must Fall.*

In 1962 the pair were found guilty of theft and malicious damage, and received fines and six months in prison for their troubles. Orton thought this was 'because we were queers'. The borough seems not to bear them any grudge, though: 41 of the results of the couple's work are displayed at the local history centre, while 31 more are thought to have been destroyed, stolen or lost.

Although Halliwell attempted suicide in prison, Orton's sentence was in some ways the artistic making of him – he could focus on writing on his own and analyse what he perceived as the hypocritical and corrupt society that his plays would seek to unsettle and satirise. Indeed, the black humour, overt sexuality and bizarre nature of his literary desecrations prefigured plays such as *Entertaining Mr Sloane* and *Loot*. A year after his release, Orton saw his first success with his radio play, *The Ruffian on the Stair*, and would go on to become one of the 20th century's most famous, internationally acclaimed playwrights. But, Orton's fame had a tragic outcome for both men: Halliwell felt threatened and isolated by his lover's success, and in 1967 murdered the 34-year-old Orton in their flat, then committed suicide.

Address Finsbury Library, 245 St John Street, EC1V 4NB, +44 (0)207 527 7988, www.islington.gov.uk | Getting there Underground to Angel (Northern line) or train or Underground to Farringdon (Hammersmith & City, and Circle lines) | Hours See website for current information on visiting; access by appointment only: email local.history@islington.gov.uk | Tip At nearby Wesley's Chapel (49 City Road, EC1Y 1AD), you can visit the home of the founder of Methodism, and the museum that tells the story of the Church from his time until the present.

44 The Isokon Building

Hampstead's modernist building

Agatha Christie (see ch. 31) wrote her only espionage novel, *N or M?*, when living in flat 20 of this striking modernist apartment block. It would be nice to think that fact and fiction mixed, as seven Soviet spies, including Arnold Deutsch, controller of the Cambridge Five spy ring, lived here in the 1930s. Christie, though, moved to the flats in 1941, at the height of the Blitz, trained as an air raid warden, and left in 1947. However, there were others, residents and visitors, whose time crossed over with Christie, whom she may have met and conversed with, such as the German communist Kuczynski family. Certainly, her novel is remarkable for its knowledge of Fifth Column activity and intelligence tradecraft during World War Two. Here, she also wrote *The Body in the Library*, *Five Little Pigs*, and *The Moving Finger*.

The Isokon Building, also known as the Lawn Road Flats, was Britain's first deck access flats with external walkways. Christie described it as looking like 'a giant liner which ought to have had a couple of funnels…'. Unsurprisingly, three members of the Bauhaus school of architecture – all refugees from the Nazis – had homes here: Walter Gropius, the founder, Marcel Breuer, designer of modernist furniture, and Laszlo Moholy-Nagy. The original 32 apartments now number 36 (what was the garage is now the Isokon Gallery). They were built between 1929 and 1932, and opened in 1936. They were constructed of reinforced concrete, and designed by Canadian engineer Wells Coates, himself a resident.

Other writers who lived here included Nicholas Monserrat, author of *The Cruel Sea* and *The Ship that Died of Shame*, E. F. Herbert, the children's book writer, and Charles Brasch, the New Zealand poet and Bletchley Park intelligence officer. The cultural milieu was added to by the sculptors Henry Moore, Barbara Hepworth and the painter Ben Nicholson, all of whom lived nearby.

Address Isokon Gallery, Lawn Lane, NW3 2XD, www.isokongallery.org | **Getting there** Underground to Belsize Park (Northern line) | **Hours** Gallery: Mar–Oct, Sat & Sun 11am–4pm; visit www.programme.openhouse.co.uk for tours | **Tip** One of Hampstead Heath's little known charms is The Pergola overlooking West Heath. It was created by Lord Leverhulme, industrialist and philanthropist and Thomas Mawson, the landscape architect. The associated Hill Garden was once a private garden.

45 Keats House

A poet's medical notes

Like some other writers – most famously, Somerset Maugham (see ch. 92) and Arthur Conan Doyle (see ch. 79) – London-born John Keats trained as a doctor, in his case as a surgeon-apothecary at Guy's Hospital Medical School from 1815 to 1816. He left school at the age of 14 to become apprenticed to the family doctor, Thomas Hammond, in Edmonton, before registering as a medical student at the hospital. Despite only a year in this position, Keats seems to have enjoyed his period at Guy's: he dressed in the style of Byron, developed a taste for claret, snuff and cigars, played billiards, and attended boxing matches, cockfights and bear-baiting. But his days were long and demanding.

Keats' medical notebook was given to the Borough of Hampstead in 1911 by Sir Charles Wentworth Dilke, grandson of Keats' friend of the same name, and was transferred to Keats House in 1924. He wrote in a small leather-bound notebook to record lectures. His name appears neatly inscribed on the inside front cover. While his anatomy notes are neat and well structured, those on physiology are written quickly, sometimes sketchily, haphazard, idiosyncratic and at an angle, with abbreviations and spelling errors. As Keats missed several lectures, his notes are non-sequential: the first four lectures are recorded at the beginning of the book, the next twelve at the end, and other lectures are fitted in throughout. Doodles of flowers lie near a description of how to treat a dislocated jaw, while fruits and skulls decorate the margins!

Although he showed a natural aptitude for medicine, throughout his training Keats also dedicated himself to writing. Not long after gaining an apothecary's licence he gave up medicine, partly to concentrate on poetry, but also afraid of making the surgical errors common at that time. A statue in the hospital's grounds commemorates his abortive career.

Address 10 Keats Grove, NW3 2RR, +44 (0)2 7332 3868, www.cityoflondon.gov.uk | Getting there Overground to Hampstead Heath | Hours Thu, Fri & Sun 11am – 1pm & 2 – 4pm | Tip Visit nearby Well Walk for the fountain that made the Chalybeate Well what it was – a philanthropic gift to the area's poor in 1698, when the local springs had supposed healing properties.

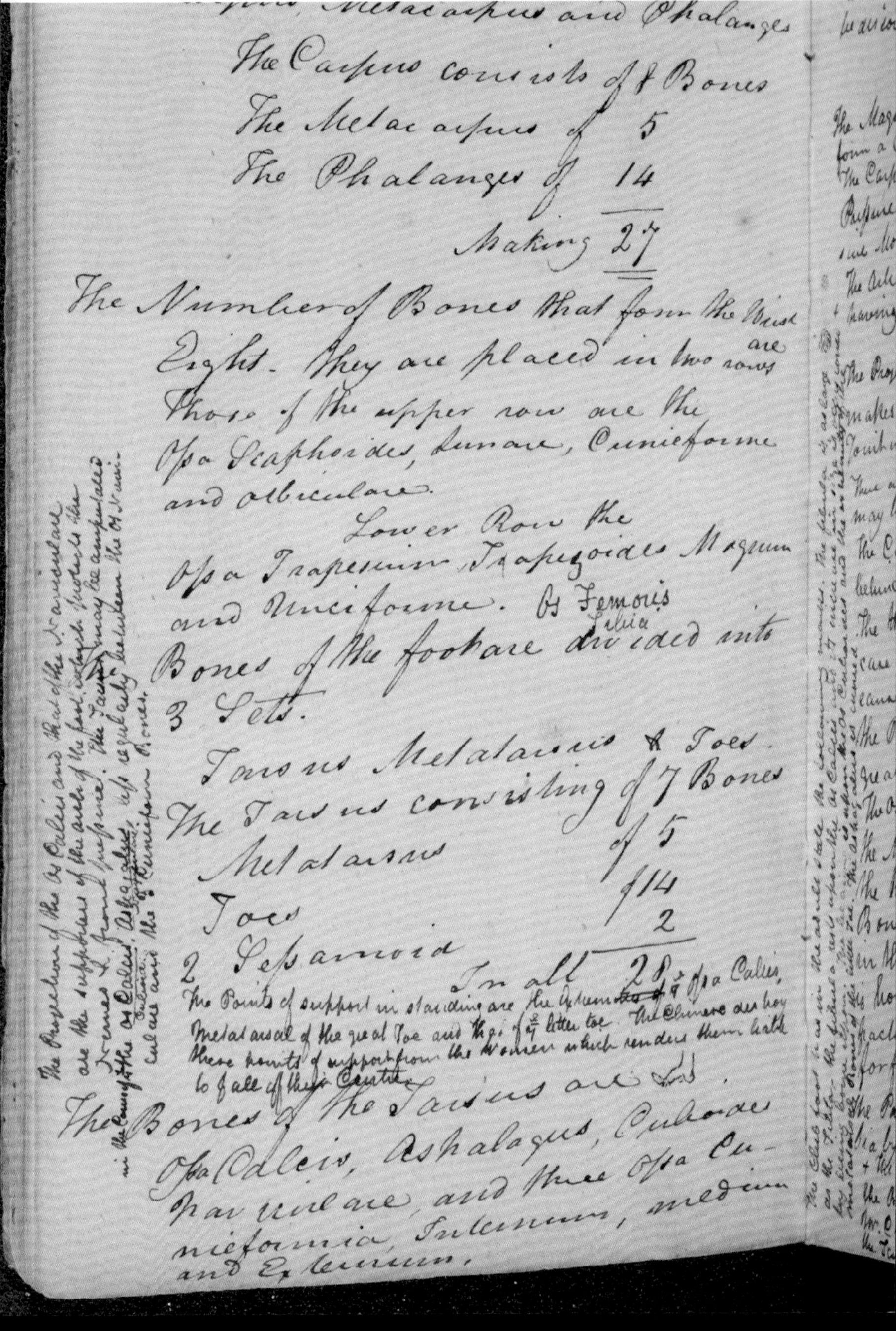

Metacarpus and Phalanges
The Carpus consists of 8 Bones
The Metacarpus of 5
The Phalanges of 14
Making 27
The Number of Bones that form the Wrist
Eight. They are placed in two rows
those of the upper row are the
Ossa Scaphoides, Lunare, Cuneiforme
and Orbiculare.
Lower Row the
Ossa Trapezium, Trapezoides Magnum
and Unciforme.
Bones of the foot are divided into
3 Sets.
Tarsus Metatarsus & Toes.
The Tarsus consisting of 7 Bones
Metatarsus of 5
Toes of 14
2 Sesamoid 2
In all 28
The Bones of the Tarsus are
Ossa Calcis, Astragalus, Cuboides
Naviculare, and three Ossa Cuneiformia, Internum, medium
and Externum.

46 Kensington Gardens

Inspiration for Peter Pan

The Peter Pan statue in Kensington Gardens commemorates not its subject's creator, J. M. Barrie, but his most famous fictional character. Barrie moved from Nottingham, where he had worked as a journalist, to London in 1883, at the age of 23. He settled at 100 Bayswater Road, opposite the park. He became well known for his sketches of life in his native Scotland, and after moving to No. 100 (as it was then) Leinster Corner, his plays *Quality Street* and *The Admirable Crichton*. However, author and subject had another personal connection: Peter Pan was inspired by Barrie's brother, David, who had died at the age of 13. Barrie's heartbroken mother saw David as a boy who would never grow up and leave her.

Barrie would walk in Kensington Gardens to relax and think. It was on one such foray that he met George, Peter, John, Michael, and Nicholas, the five sons of Arthur and Sylvia Llewellyn-Davies, when they were walking in the park with their nurse. When in 1904 Barrie turned his 1902 fantasy, *The Little White Bird*, into a successful play, *Peter Pan, the Boy who Wouldn't Grow Up*, Peter Pan was joined by John and Michael (with Wendy), as Barrie named his characters, as members of the Darling family. *Peter Pan in Kensington Gardens* followed in 1906. He wrote these works in a stable-cum-garage at the bottom of his garden. Meanwhile, Barrie became infatuated with Sylvia, sister of the actor Gerald du Maurier; this, coupled with his wife's affair with a young actor, led to their divorce in 1902 – a very unusual and even sensational event at the time.

The statue is located at the spot where Peter lands after his journey from Neverland. Its origins feed quite deliberately into the myth of Peter Pan. It was erected one night in April 1912, in the belief that early morning walkers and visitors would think that 'the boy who never grew up' had arrived by magic.

Address W2 4RU, +44 (0)300 061 2000, www.royalparks.org.uk | Getting there Underground to Lancaster Gate (Central line) | Hours Unrestricted | Tip Queen Victoria's elaborate and overpowering tribute to her husband Prince Albert is a short distance south of Peter Pan. Unveiled in 1876, the Prince Consort sits regally, cast in gilded bronze, beneath a canopy. The decoration around the statue represents progress in industry, the arts, commerce, engineering and agriculture.

47 Keynes Library

Where the West was won – by books

John Maynard Keynes' library in his former home is where he produced two of the most influential books ever written. In 1920 he published *Economic Consequences of the Peace*, which did much to ignite the criticism of the Versailles Treaty. The book, which combines economic theory with often critical portraits of the peacemakers, was written as a result of Keynes' attending the Versailles Peace Conference in 1919 for six months after the First World War. Paris was dispiriting for him, with the penalties imposed by the victors on the defeated. In 1936 came his *General Theory of Employment, Interest and Money*. This laid the foundations of what became known as Keynesianism, a shorthand for deficit financing, government intervention, and economic planning, which continues to influence Western economic thinking.

Keynes first moved into No. 40 – part of what is now Birkbeck College's School of Arts – in 1916 as a tenant of the art critic Clive Bell, and his wife, the painter Vanessa Bell. She and her siblings, including Virginia Woolf, had previously lived there. Keynes took over the lease in 1918. The Bells retained rooms for a while, but Keynes and Bell, who could express himself coarsely, were not always the most agreeable of co-habitees.

Keynes worked at the Treasury, and in 1924 became bursar of King's College, Cambridge. His writings led to his leading the British delegation in 1944 to the conference that led to the setting up of the International Monetary Fund, based in part on his proposals in the 1920 book.

Bell called the house – somewhat self-aggrandisingly – the Bloomsbury group's 'monument historique'. The library has many of the aspects – including three large canvasses by Vanessa – that Keynes would have known. He remained here until his death in 1946, after which his widow, the ballerina Lydia Lopokova, lived here for another two years.

Address 43 Gordon Square, WC1H 0PD, +44 (0)20 3926 2642, www.bbk.ac.uk | Getting there Underground to Russell Square (Piccadilly line) | Hours Viewing from outside only | Tip In 1913 5,000 suffragettes followed the funeral cortege for a brief service for Emily Wilding Davison at St George's Church, 10 minutes' walk south. A suffragette, she died when she jumped in front of the king's horse at The Derby, and was buried in Morpeth, Northumberland.

48 Lambeth Palace Library

The first printed book in Britain

Go to the gift shop in Lambeth Palace Library and you'll find plenty of books for sale, just as there are in other museums, galleries and bookshops within easy reach of the library. But this particular place is home to a book that's the ancestor of all others, from Shakespeare to Harry Potter, Agatha Christie (see ch. 31) to Dickens (see ch. 19): the Gutenberg Bible.

This bible was the first printed book in English – the beginning of the so-called 'Gutenberg revolution', or the beginning of the printed book in the West. It was created in Mainz by Johann Gutenberg in the mid-1450s. Around that time a young man, who later became Pope Pius II, mentioned it to the cardinal for whom he worked, in what was the first reference to a printed book. Either 150 or 180 copies had been produced, he said, with lettering so clear that his eminence would be able to read it without his glasses.

Printed bibles were not as widely used in churches as later; rather, there were extracts in missals. This Gutenberg is not complete, containing only the New Testament, as do most of the surviving first Gutenbergs. A note scribbled in English of no later than 1500 indicates that this version came to England early. It is further dated by the fact that the extensive exquisite hand-painted decoration by a 15th century English artist was probably added not long after 1455. Thus, this may be the first book ever to arrive in Britain.

This version, too, is unusual in that there is no decoration in some copies, or on only a few pages. Printed on vellum, not paper, a painted initial and decoration heads every significant text. The unknown original owner is likely to have purchased it for a religious house in return for prayer. Only in 1789 did bibliophiles search for which edition Gutenberg had printed. This one was at Lambeth and catalogued for a long time before being identified in 1873.

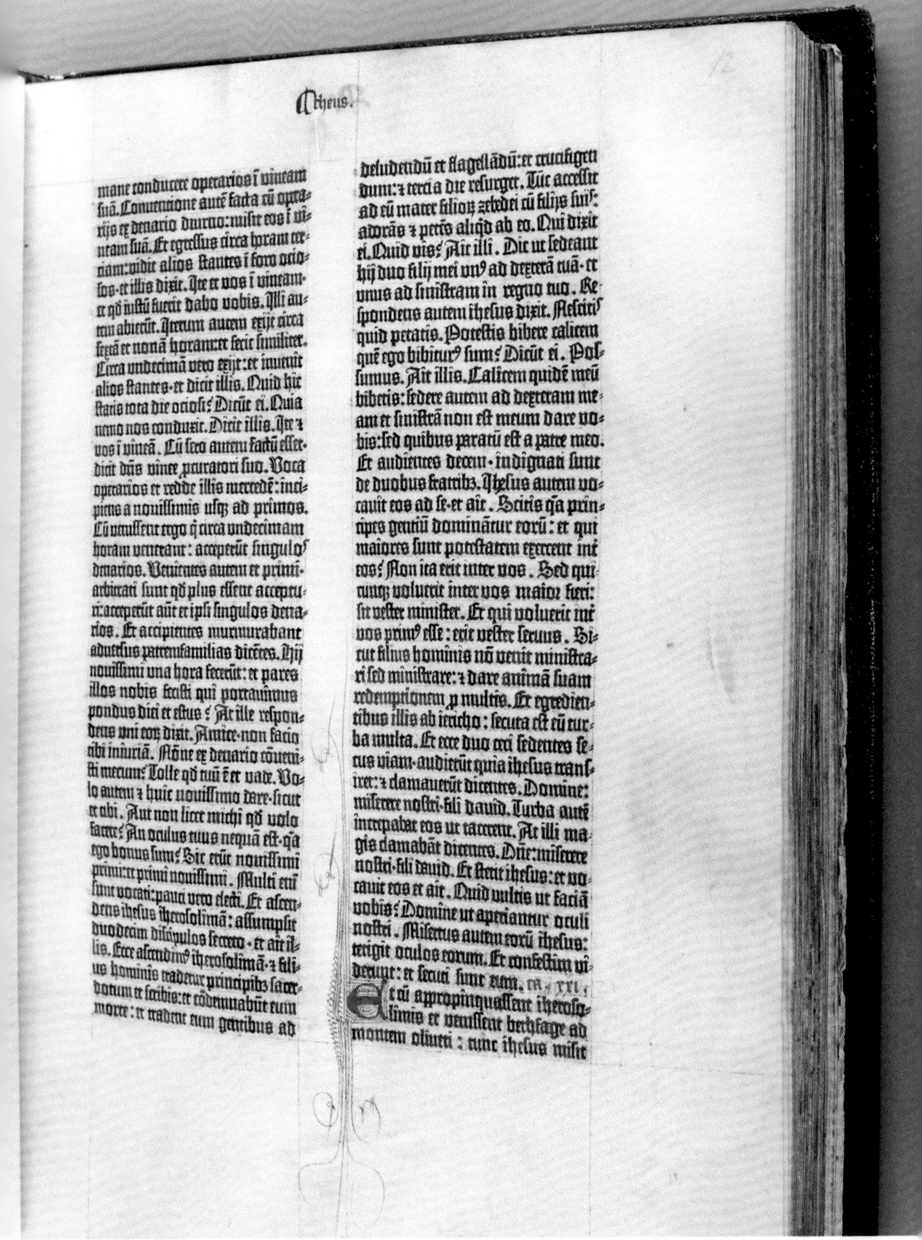

Address 17 Lambeth Palace Road, SE1 7JT, +44 (0)207 898 1400, www.lambethpalacelibrary.org | **Getting there** Underground to Westminster (Circle, District and Jubilee lines) and Lambeth North (Bakerloo line) | **Hours** See website for current information on visiting | **Tip** The Garden Museum can be found in St Mary's Church. The museum explains the design and history of gardens, with three exhibitions a year and a permanent collection of garden ephemera.

49 Lancaster Gate

Muriel Spark's girls of 'slender means'

In 1944 Muriel Spark left her native Edinburgh for London to establish a literary career, but also she wanted, as she said, 'to experience the war'. Her home for many years would be Helena House, at 82 Lancaster Gate: a hostel founded by a daughter of Queen Victoria. Spark found it 'absolutely charming', looking out, as it did, across Kensington Gardens to the Albert Memorial. It was 'very spacious with an air of quiet but expensive elegance at odds with the humble price we paid'. Her room, at the top of the house, cost her 12s 6d (65p) a week; lunch was 2s 6d (13p). There were maids to clean and make the beds, a large drawing room, and a music room in which to practise.

Her first novel wasn't published until 1957, and in 1963 she immortalised the club in her seventh novel, *The Girls of Slender Means*, as the May of Teck Club, with the detail she had known. Helena House's founding purpose was for 'Ladies of Good Families of Modest Means who are Obliged to Pursue an Occupation in London', mirrored in the May of Teck being 'for the Pecuniary Convenience and Social Protection of Ladies of Slender Means under the age of Thirty Years...'.

The novel's 40 girls reflect the residents of Spark's time: they are middle class from 'good families' – clergymen's daughters and secretaries, some working in government, some in publishing. They fall in and out of love; dress for dinner; celebrate the war's end; suffer post-war rationing. Some share rooms, while others, like Spark, have a room to themselves. Some are in their late teens, a few are older, long-time fixtures in the club. The short novel begins comically but has a tragic climax (not experienced by Spark and her fellows). It is a portrait of a place and time, about which Spark received an 'affectionate' letter from Mrs G. S. Taylor, the warden in her time, who was happy to recognise Helena House in the novel.

Address 82 Lancaster Gate, W2 2HH | Getting there Underground to Lancaster Gate (Central line) | Hours Viewable from outside only | Tip Just to the south is The Serpentine Gallery, more accurately, Serpentine South and Serpentine North – two galleries linked by a bridge, which offer some of the most interesting examples of contemporary art (www.serpentinegalleries.org).

50_The London Library

Tiny books in a very large collection

The London Library's collection of miniature books contains nearly 350 titles printed between the 16th and 20th centuries, all of which are under five inches high. The collection includes books by Thomas More printed in 1610, a book of psalms from 1534, collections of James Joyce's poetry, and an original 1839 copy of *Bradshaw's Guide* – the world's first railway timetable. Also to be found on the shelves are miniatures (defined as books under three inches high), printed mostly in the 19th century – said to be the golden age of miniature printing. The 'Fly's Eye Dante' of 1878 is the smallest version of Dante's *Divina Commedia* in the world, while the smallest Authorised Version of the Bible, printed by David Bryce of Glasgow in 1896, comes with its own magnifying glass.

The library has been distinguished since its foundation in May 1841, above a former gambling den at 49 Pall Mall, when Thomas Carlyle, frustrated by the lack of lending libraries, private or otherwise, in London, gathered support for what is now one of the world's great literary institutions. There were 382 founding subscribers. The first 2,000 books were hand-picked by future prime minister William Gladstone, the philosopher John Stuart Mill, and the Italian revolutionary Giuseppe Mazzini. Prince Albert gave £50 and a number of books, and became the library's first patron.

Among the first members were scientist Charles Darwin (see ch. 28), writer Harriet Martineau, and novelist Charles Dickens (see ch. 19). Since then, most well-known authors – historians, novelists, biographers, five poets laureate and eleven Nobel Prize winners – have been members, and worked among the shelves. The library moved to its present home in 1845. Today there are more than one million books, dating from 1580, covering 2,000 subjects in 55 languages, as well as bound copies of 2,000 periodicals dating from 1699.

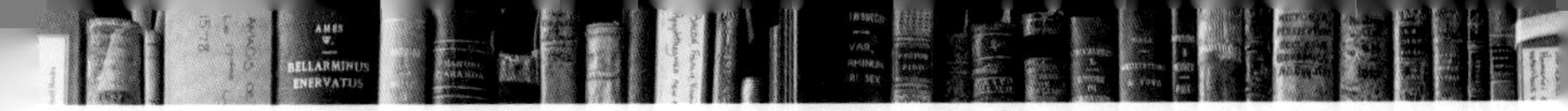

Address 14 St James Square, SW1Y 4LG, +44 (0)207 766 4700, www.londonlibrary.co.uk | Getting there Underground to Green Park (Jubilee, Piccadilly and Victoria lines) or Piccadilly Circus (Bakerloo and Piccadilly lines) | Hours Mon–Tue 9.30am–9pm, Wed–Fri 9.30am–5.30pm, Sat 9.30am–5.30pm; a fee of £20 allows daily membership to view anywhere; informal short tours are also available | Tip Walk left along Pall Mall and then right again at the Athenaeum, and at the bottom on the right by the Duke of York Steps you'll find the grave of 'Giro', the pet terrier of Nazi and former Weimar ambassador, Leopold von Hoesch.

51 London Zoo

Lear, no-nonsense illustrator

At 15, a largely uneducated Edward Lear was keeping himself as a painter of screens and making anatomical drawings. But what first brought him recognition was not the limericks and nonsense verses for which he is now best known, but work he found as an illustrator at the London Zoo. Opened in Regent's Park in 1826 as a centre for research, three years later, when animals from existing zoos were moved to it, the public were admitted.

A wealthy friend and admirer of Lear's drawings got him an introduction and he was allowed to draw parrots. Two of his drawings – a lemur and two macaws – appeared in a zoo publication. His own publication, *Illustrations of the Family of Pisscitacidae, or Parrots*, appeared in parts between 1830 and 1832 – and in book form that latter year – privately published with 175 subscriptions. The publication, with its almost photographic representations, was unusual for several reasons: it was devoted to one bird family, published in a large format and printed lithographically, and was the first in which the artist worked from nature. The day after publication, Lear was recommended for associate membership of the Linnean Society.

Slow payment by subscribers forced Lear to abandon the project and work as an illustrator for others. Taken on by the Earl of Derby to work at his private menagerie at Knowsley Hall, there he also wrote his first book of limericks for publication, having written nonsense verse since childhood.

Lear spent decades abroad, becoming a successful landscape painter and water colourist, but continued to write the limericks and nonsense verses that have given him enduring fame. His *Book of Nonsense* came out anonymously in 1846, and has been in print ever since. Now seen as one of the greatest of ornithological illustrators, Lear's limericks and nonsense poems often feature birds and animals.

Address Outer Circle, NW1 4RY, +44 (0)344 225 1826, www.zsl.org | Getting there Underground to Camden Town (Northern line) or Overground to Camden Road | Hours See website for current information on visiting | Tip A short walk on your way to the zoo is Camden Lock (www.camdenmarket.com) one of the capital's first crafts and antiques markets, begun in 1974. Now there are all kinds of independent shops and stalls to see – and you can take a boat trip up the Regent's Canal.

Salmon-crested Cockatoo ⅔ Nat Size

52 Marble Hill House

Pope as Grand Gardener at Thameside mansion

Alexander Pope's translation of *The Odyssey* and *The Iliad* brought him fame, establishing his lasting reputation as a poet. But two words – Plumb bush – in fading brown ink on the manuscript of *The Iliad*, allowed him to be identified in 2018, 274 years after his death, as the part-creator of the great garden of his friend Henrietta Howard, Countess of Suffolk, at her home at Marble Hill House.

In 'On a certain lady at court', Pope spoke of her 'equal Mixture of good Humour/And sensible soft Melancholy'. She had been mistress to George II, and when he moved on to a new mistress, a settlement enabled the twice-widowed Howard to buy the 25 acres of land at Marble Hill, now in 66 acres of riverside parkland. It was known that Pope had overseen the landscaping, with the professional gardener, Charles Bridgeman. (He had been 'extremely busie' with landscaping in 1726 at the Earl of Oxford's estate in Cambridgeshire.)

However, 'Plum bush' linked that knowledge to the actual garden designs, which were on the back of old sheets of paper which he used when making his translation. They were believed to be the plans for Howard's garden, but there was no proof until it was realised that Plum bush was the name of an old field for part of her estate whose many features match those on a map of the garden discovered in Howard's papers. These include meandering paths intended to recall the shady groves of classical literature, while a rare 18th-century nine-pin bowling alley has also been excavated. English Heritage is restoring the garden, although the terraces, woodland areas and the oval lawn, grotto and ice house are all that remain.

The Palladian mansion, managed by English Heritage, was built at the same time as the garden's creation and became the permanent home of Howard, surrounded by an intellectual circle which included Pope and John Gay, the poet and dramatist.

Address Richmond Road, TW1 2NL, +44 (0)20 8892 5115, www.english-heritage.org.uk | Getting there Train to St Margarets | Hours Daily 10am–5pm; park: 6.30am–6.30pm | Tip The home of the painter J. M. W. Turner, Sandycombe Lodge, is a few minutes' walk away. This Grade II-listed house is of a picturesque-cottage style, designed by Turner and built in 1813 as his country retreat.

53 Marx Memorial Library

More than a memorial to Marx

Two events in 1933 brought the Marx Memorial Library into being: the 50th anniversary of the death of Karl Marx, and the public burning of books by the Nazis in Berlin. But this handsome Grade II-listed building has a far longer history than the library it now houses, or even of Marxism.

It was founded in 1738 as a Welsh charity school. The school moved out in 1772 to be succeeded by workshops when the building was divided, partly to become the home of the London Patriotic Society from 1872 until 1892. A radical printer took over, and the building returned to single occupancy. In 1826, the writer William Corbett made his speech against the Corn Laws on the green.

Many well-known writers and radicals are associated with the library: William Morris (see ch. 110) was an early benefactor, while Lenin had an office here (which can still be seen) when editing the revolutionary Russian-language newspaper *The Spark* from 1902 to 1903. This was printed on especially thin paper to enable it to be smuggled into Russia.

The library's cultural and educational remit roams further than its name may suggest. Its library has 50,000 books, pamphlets and periodicals on matters from Marxism to the anti-apartheid struggle, the Peasants' Revolt of 1381 to the Poll Tax protests of the 1980s. Extensive archives relate to the International Brigade in the Spanish Civil War, and the print unions. There are 1,600 posters, and, in addition to lectures, online learning is also available. Over the years, the library – originally with the suffix 'and Workers' School' – has expanded to fill the whole building. One treasure of the library is a mural – 'The worker of the future clearing away the chaos of capitalism' – painted in 1934 by the Communist Viscount Hastings, who studied under the Mexican artist Diego Rivera. It was discovered behind a bookcase.

Address 37a Clerkenwell Green, EC1R 0DU, +44 (0)207 253 1485, www.marx-memorial-library.org.uk | **Getting there** Overground or Underground to Farringdon (Circle, Hammersmith & City, and Metropolitan lines) | **Hours** Tours Mon at 12pm; reading room Tue–Thu 11am–4pm, by appointment | **Tip** The Charterhouse in Charterhouse Square, EC1M 6AN is on an ancient monastic site. It has been a private mansion, a school, and is now a residential care home. Its long and diverse history is shown in its museum, for which tours are available (www.thecharterhouse.org).

54 Middle Temple

Where law meets literature

Middle Temple summons up the law. And quite right, too – it is one of the four Inns of Court that promote and support the rule of law and its fair and effective administration throughout the Common Law world. But Middle Temple has had another, far less well-known life – that of literature.

During the 17th century, it was common for law students in the Middle Temple to organise and act in masques and plays in the Hall, which remains the centre of the Middle Temple. Revelry around Christmas sometimes lasted from All Saints' Eve to Candlemas Day. There were celebrations, riotous feasting, drinking, dancing, and processions. Candlemas Feast 1602 is particularly notable. While no Middle Temple records survive, a student, John Manningham, noted in his diary the first known performance of Shakespeare's *Twelfth Night* in the Hall. Actors are not mentioned, but it is possible that the author himself was one of them.

Middle Temple was in this period sometimes referred to as 'the third university' after Oxford and Cambridge, since the young men, who were wealthy and socially well connected, who studied to qualify in the law occupied this elite place. Student lawyers lived and worked as 'members' at an inn of court, and often frequented the nearby indoor theatres. While notable Middle Templars very obviously include distinguished lawyers, its members also include famous writers, among them the diarist John Evelyn, the playwright William Congreve, the novelists John Buchan and Charles Dickens (see ch. 19), and latter-day historians, Cecily (C. V.) Wedgwood and Lisa Jardine.

The library, designed by 20th-century architect Edward Maufe, holds approximately 250,000 volumes, covering all aspects of British, European and American law, as well as the its archives, and a collection of rare antiquarian books. Lectures are open to non-members.

Address Middle Temple Lane, EC4Y 9AT, +44 (0)207 427 4800, www.middletemple.org.uk | Getting there Underground to Chancery Lane (Central line) or Temple (District and Circle lines) | Hours See website for current information on visiting; for tours email events@middletemple.org.uk | Tip The long-closed Aldwych Underground station is minutes away on The Strand. Official tours of this and other disused tube stations are available (www.ltmuseum.co.uk).

55 Montpelier Square

Arthur Koestler's end

While already well known for previous books, notably *Spanish Testament* (1937), it was *Darkness at Noon* in 1940, a novel about the Stalinist terror published during the purges, that gave the Hungarian-born Arthur Koestler international fame. Having joined the German Communist Party in 1931, he resigned in 1939 due to the direction of Stalin's USSR.

Koestler moved to Britain in the year his novel was published, and for the rest of his life was a prolific writer of autobiography, essays and novels, whilst also advocating a variety of causes, including the abolition of capital punishment. In 1968 he was awarded Denmark's Sonning Prize for outstanding contributions to European culture, and in 1972 became a Commander of the Order of the British Empire. But on 3 March, 1983, five years after the publication of his last book, the 78-year-old Koestler, and Christine Jeffries, his secretary, occasional lover and later third wife, killed themselves in their flat at 8 Montpelier Square.

Seven years earlier Koestler had been diagnosed with Parkinson's disease, which caused increasing physical disability. He later developed terminal leukaemia, needing daily nursing care. Having decided the previous year to take his own life, he had written a note to absolve Christine of any legal consequences. But she later added a paragraph explaining that she would die with him, as she would not want to live without him. On the fateful evening, Koestler, having written a letter to his doctor and lawyer, put on a jacket and tie. The couple then sat opposite each other in the living room, sipped whisky and wine, and chewed Tuinal tablets until they slipped into a coma and died.

They were cremated at Mortlake Crematorium. They left bequests of £1 million to establish a chair at Edinburgh University in parapsychology, a subject of increasing interest to Koestler in his later years.

Address 8 Montpelier Square, SW7 IJU | Getting there Underground to Knightsbridge (Piccadilly line) | Hours Viewable from outside only | Tip Walk in the footsteps of Charles Darwin (see ch. 28), David Attenborough and dinosaurs with a visit to the Natural History Museum. Over 80 million items set humankind within the context of the animal world (www.nhm.ac.uk).

56 National Poetry Library

Little-known literary treasury

With the National Theatre, the Hayward Gallery and the National Film Theatre, as well as many restaurants and a bookshop, it is easy to overlook the National Poetry Library in the bustle of the South Bank, even if it is on the fifth floor of another of the area's attractions: the Royal Festival Hall. Its 95,000 volumes comprise the largest modern poetry collection, and it is the largest poetry public lending library in the world, with UK stock dating from 1912. Its ever-growing collection of almost 300,000 items includes books, magazines and audio recordings, often of poets reading their own work. Much of the collection is from overseas.

Founded by the Arts Council, the library was opened in 1953 by the writer Herbert Read and the Nobel Prize winner T. S. Eliot (see ch. 76). The library has had several homes, but came to the South Bank in 1988, when another Nobel laureate, Seamus Heaney, opened this venue. In fact, Heaney and the former Poet Laureate Ted Hughes (see ch. 85) co-edited an anthology, *Rattle Bag*, and Hughes wrote of his experience of researching the book in the library, when working in its then offices in Covent Garden (the South Bank is its fifth address). He wrote of 'going through every book that showed any likelihood of producing a poem for the anthology... I was trekking for days through the densely packed Ys and the insuperably ranked Ws'. Andrew Motion, also Poet Laureate, worked in the library on his anthology, *Here to Eternity*, while Philip Larkin called the library 'pure flowerings the imagination for which the English are so seldom given credit'.

Now in its 50th year, membership is free and 18,000 books are loaned each a year. This is a testament to the library's belief that poetry is for everyone, whether those 'who can't live without it', families and children, academics, teachers, researchers, the curious – and, of course, poets themselves.

Address Level 5, Royal Festival Hall, Southbank Centre, Belvedere Road, SE1 8XX, +44 (0)207 921 0943, www.nationalpoetrylibrary.org.uk | Getting there Train to Waterloo or Underground to Waterloo (Bakerloo, Northern, Jubilee, and Waterloo & City lines) | Hours Tue noon – 6pm, Wed – Sun noon – 8pm | Tip Apart from all the other cultural attractions on the South Bank, don't neglect the open air book market under Southwark Bridge, offering a huge selection that ranges from biographies to modern and classic fiction, music and art, as well as old prints.

57 National Portrait Gallery

Jane Austen's only true likeness

Jane Austen is one of the most popular novelists of all time, and one of the greatest women writers. Yet despite her popularity we have little idea what she really looked like. Every Jane Austen reader has their own image of the author, but the only portrait authenticated as a true likeness is an unflattering, pencil and watercolour sketch in the National Portrait Gallery.

The sketch was made in 1810, when Jane was 31, by her older sister, Cassandra. This was seven years before the sister's death, and she had yet to write her six novels. Although Cassandra was a painter, the portrait does not show an obviously outstanding talent, and the Jane depicted is at odds with its sociable and good-humoured subject: she and her siblings – she also had six brothers – were in much demand at dances at country houses. Here, though, she looks rather grumpy and unsmiling. This is not the only portrait of Jane by Cassandra. Another was made at Lyme Regis, but shows its subject in back view, her face hidden by a bonnet.

It was perhaps appropriate that Cassandra, practical and self-confident, should have made the sketch, for she and Jane were the closest of sisters. Cassandra looked upon Jane as 'wiser and better' than herself, and was her confidante. Neither of the women married, and they lived together during their adult lives, with Cassandra nursing Jane through her final illness.

The NPG portrait came to light after a search by the family for an illustration for the memoir by Jane's nephew, James Edward Austen-Leigh, published in 1870. The way in which Jane was portrayed did not accord with her family's memories, and some members complained to Edward after the book's publication. The portrait came into the gallery's possession in 1948. It is unfortunate that the portrait's unflattering likeness of Jane Austen is the one forever associated with its subject.

Address St Martin's Place, London, WC2H 0HE, +44 (0)207 306 0055, www.npg.org.uk | Getting there Underground to Charing Cross (Bakerloo and Northern lines) or Embankment (District, Circle, Northern and Bakerloo lines) | Hours Sun–Thu 10.30am–6pm, Fri & Sat 10.30am–9pm | Tip On the south side of Trafalgar Square is a police lookout disguised as one of two large granite pillars supporting lanterns. The one on the eastern side was hollowed out and made accessible to allow discreet observation of political demonstrations, but modern communications and technology have since made this lookout redundant.

58 Newington Green

'The birthplace of feminism'

One of the oldest Unitarian meeting houses in the country, with ties to political radicalism going back more than 300 years to its opening in 1708, Newington Green's most famous minister was Dr Richard Price. It was partly Price's ministry that attracted Mary Wollstonecraft to the congregation. His sermons inspired her work, in arguing for the new French republic and about the rights of women. Wollstonecraft, who went on to publish *A Vindication of the Rights of Women* in 1792, is commemorated by a mural on the side of the church.

However, Wollstonecraft's introduction to feminism came earlier. When living in east London, she read John Locke's view that a husband 'should have no more power' over his wife than 'she had over his life'. This was a time when hitting a wife was legal, when women had no property rights or the right to vote, and children were the husband's 'property'. In 1786, while running a failing girls' school in an effort to do something about the poor future prospects for girls, and which she moved to Newington Green, she wrote her *Thoughts on the Education of Daughters*, which earned her £10.

Wollstonecraft died in 1797, giving birth to another renowned feminist and author, Mary Shelley, future author of *Frankenstein*. In 2020, a sculpture of Wollstonecraft by Maggie Hambling was unveiled on the green. It differs from previous representations, which have Wollstonecraft often in loose-fitting drapes and sometimes wearing a hat. Hambling's work is classical in tone, with its subject as an idealised nude figure rather than a sculpted likeness. In this representation, it is her heroism that is on display rather than her likeness. Around the base are inscribed Wollstonecraft's words, 'I do not wish that women have power over men, but over themselves'. Controversial, Hambling said it was a representation of every woman rather than Wollstonecraft herself.

Address 39A Newington Green, Newington Green, N16 9PR, +44 (0)207 354 0774, www.ngmeeting.house | **Getting there** Overground to Canonbury | **Hours** See website for current information on visiting, guided tours (must be booked in advance) and services | **Tip** Old St Mary's Church on Stoke Newington Church Street is now an arts venue, but also used for worship; it's a rare example of an Elizabethan church, with medieval origins, and a reminder of when this busy part of London was a rural village (www.stmaryn16.org).

59 New Inn Broadway

London's first theatre

Most visitors looking for the site of The Theatre, said by the author Richard Shapiro to be 'London's oldest and most celebrated', will find a plaque in Curtain Road. It states that The Theatre, the first built since Roman times, in 1567, was to the east of the plaque – though no exact location is given. In fact, it is only a short walk away in New Inn Broadway, which is, despite its name, a narrow back street. An inscription set into the pavement says that this is where The Theatre was located. This is emphasised by a statue of Shakespeare, an early performer, seated on a bench, and three of the nearby seven granite blocks inscribed with his words.

The City of London authorities passed a law to prevent any theatre being built within the Square Mile, believing that theatres were places of disorder. James Burbage, the actor-manager, decided, in association with his brother-in-law John Brayne, to build The Theatre, which would be within easy reach of Londoners. Ben Jonson's plays were staged there, as some of Shakespeare's may have been.

Two excavations performed in recent years where The Theatre once stood, have shown that it existed within a large complex, polygonal in shape, and was likely constructed of timber. It had capacity for 1,500 people, seated in three levels of galleries around an open yard.

The venture ended when Burbage and Brayne, indicted in 1571 for 'tumults leading to a breach of the peace' caused by showing 'playes or interludes', fell out over Burbage's alleged financial double-dealing. The lease expired in 1597, the year of Burbage's death, after which the building was dismantled by his sons, Cuthbert and Richard – himself one of the most celebrated of actors – and 12 workmen. They transported the materials in carts, using them to build The Globe Theatre on the South Bank, now replaced by the modern replica of the same name.

Address EC2A 3PR | Getting there Overground to Shoreditch High Street and Liverpool Street, or train or Underground to Liverpool Street (Central, Circle, Hammersmith & City, Elizabeth and Metropolitan lines) | Hours Unrestricted | Tip A 20-minute walk into the City of London will take you to the 202ft Monument on Fish Street Hill marking the spot where, in a baker's shop on Pudding Lane, the Great Fire of London broke out in 1666.

60 Notre Dame de France

A poet paints the walls

Notre Dame de France, a minute from the bustle of Leicester Square, was consecrated in 1868 to cater for 'the lower class French', who then lived in Soho. It was largely rebuilt in the mid-1950s due to war-time bombing damage. It's appropriate, then, that in the new Lady Chapel are three murals painted in 1959 by the great French poet, writer and film maker, Jean Cocteau. They depict scenes in the life of the Virgin Mary: the Annunciation, the Crucifixion and the Assumption. He painted them in gratitude for an honorary doctorate from Oxford University, and they are the only ones of their kind by him outside France. They include his signature, added in 1960, and a self-portrait on the right-hand side of the crucifixion scene.

Renowned for his plays (*La Voix Humaine*), novels (*Les Enfants Terribles*), poems, and films (*Orpheus*), Cocteau was one of the leading figures in the Surrealist and Dadaist movements. The murals rely on neither movement, but are far from the classical depictions of New Testament scenes: they are realist, but quite unlike traditional devotional art, and based on lines and muted colours.

Cocteau spent just over a week in November 1959 on the work. His films were enjoying great popularity in London at the time, and thus he did not want to be distracted by unwelcome visitors. He arrived at around 10am each morning, and began by lighting a candle at the nearby statue of Our Lady of Lourdes. He appeared to talk to his characters as he created them. This, and the actual act of creation, made what the church describes as 'a dialogue' with the wall of the chapel. As Cocteau drew the Annunciation, he was heard to say joyfully to the Virgin, 'Oh, most beautiful and loveliest of God's creatures. You were the best loved so I want you to be my best piece of work, too... I am drawing you with light strokes ... You are the yet unfinished work of Grace'.

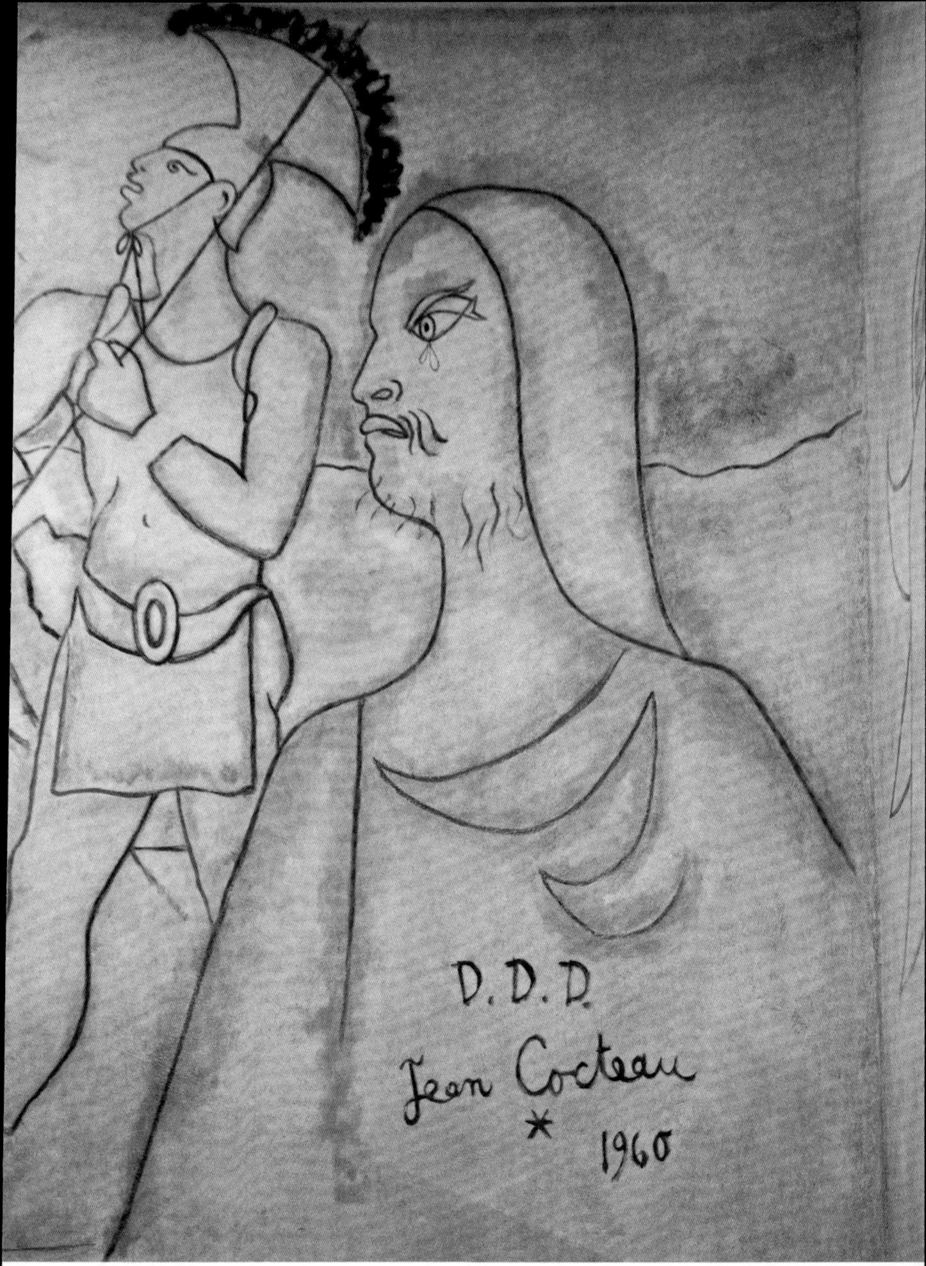

Address 5 Leicester Place, WC2H 7BX, +44 (0)207 437 9363, www.ndfchurch.org | Getting there Underground to Leicester Square (Piccadilly and Northern lines) or Piccadilly (Bakerloo and Piccadilly lines) | Hours Mon & Wed – Fri 9.30am – 9pm; see website for other opening times, masses and other services | Tip Once the site of music halls and now of several cinemas, Leicester Square commemorates culture with two rare statues: one of Shakespeare, which, with its fountain, dating from 1874, and one of Charlie Chaplin from 1981.

61 Old Bailey

Literature in the dock

Of all the notable trials that have taken place in Court Room 1 in the Old Bailey (correctly the Central Criminal Court), none has had so great a cultural effect as that in 1960 against Penguin Books, for alleged obscenity in *Lady Chatterley's Lover*. The prosecution of D. H. Lawrence's penultimate novel came 30 years after the author's death (see ch. 72). The book was first published in Italy and France in the 1920s, with an expurgated version appearing in the USA and Britain in 1932. At the trial the publishers were prosecuted under the 1959 Obscene Publications Act, which became law with (ironically) the intention of allowing works of literary merit to be published without fear of being banned because of alleged obscenity.

The book tells of the love affair between the young Lady Constance Chatterley, whose husband is paralysed through wounds received during the First World War, and her gamekeeper, Oliver Mellors. With explicit sexual scenes and the use of four-letter words, the book also explores the relationship between an upper class woman and a working class man. An array of eminent witnesses appeared for the defence, among them E. M. Forster, the novelist, Richard Hoggart, the writer and sociologist, the child psychologist Dr James Hemming and John Robinson, the Bishop of Woolwich. That Britain was changing was given comical confirmation when the prosecuting counsel, Mervyn Griffith-Jones QC, asked the jury if it were the kind of book 'you would wish your wife or servants to read'.

The novel sold 200,000 copies on the first day of its British publication, and the trial made Lawrence, already a major author, a household name even for those who had previously never heard of him. There had been obscenity trials before, but here the successful outcome opened the way for greater freedom of expression, allowing largely untrammelled explicit content for authors and publishers.

Address Central Criminal Court, Old Bailey, EC4M 7EH, +44 (0)207 192 2739, www.old-bailey.com | Getting there Underground to St Paul's (Central line) | Hours Court sits Mon–Fri 10am–1pm, 2–4.30pm; free access to public galleries; email info@oldbaileyinsight.co.uk | Tip South of the Old Bailey on Black Friars Lane is the oldest livery company hall, the impressive Apothecaries' Hall. The company was founded in 1617, and the hall rebuilt in 1672 after the Great Fire of London.

62 Paddington Station

Michael Bond's Peruvian bear found by the Browns

Paddington Station gives its name to the hapless bear from Peru, when he is found there and adopted by the Brown family. He is carrying a suitcase and has a label around his neck: 'Please look after this bear. Thank you.' The author, Michael Bond, based his creation partly on his impractical father, and partly on a teddy bear seen in Selfridge's on Christmas Eve, 1959. He bought the bear as a present for his wife, and wrote his first book in 10 days, saying he was inspired by watching children, with their bags and labels, being evacuated during wartime when he was a child.

Other people Bond had known also find expression in his characters: when he worked for the BBC monitoring unit at Caversham, Berkshire, he met Russians and Poles, whom he fed into Mr Gruber, Paddington's friend and a refugee from Hungary, who runs an antique shop on the Portobello Road.

The station is not the only London location known to Paddington. He visits Buckingham Palace to watch the changing of the guard; with the Browns and Mr Gruber he goes to Oxford Street to see the Christmas lights; and is also taken to Westminster Abbey. 'The Porchester' is the Dorchester Hotel, where Paddington is taken for a birthday treat and orders marmalade sandwiches and custard, much to the staff's bemusement. There is an outdoor performance in Hyde Park of Schubert's *Unfinished Symphony*, which the bear attempts to finish. In 'a waxworks museum' (obviously Madam Tussaud's) there is a chase through the Chamber of Horrors, while in Fortnum & Mason's in Piccadilly, Paddington wishes he were an assistant in – where else? – the marmalade department.

But for all of this, the little bear is forever associated with Paddington Station, not only because of his adopted name, but a bronze statue under the clock on platform 1 that commemorates this critical moment in his life.

Address Praed Street, W2 1RH, +(0)345 711 4141, www.networkrail.co.uk | Getting there Underground to Paddington (Bakerloo, District and Circle lines) or train to Paddington | Hours Open 24 hours | Tip Look closer at nearby 23-24 Leinster Gardens and you'll see that this elegant terrace is actually a façade built to match the houses on either side. It hides the stretch of rail track constructed for the Metropolitan line in 1863, where trains used to 'vent off' to keep the tunnels free from smoke and steam.

63 Palmers Green

Poetry from suburbia

Stevie Smith would be surprised that a memorial in her honour should stand in the centre of Palmers Green, when she may well have thought, to use her most quoted poem, that she was often 'not waving but drowning' in her many years there. Hers was a life of mixed professional fortunes, much of it spent in the obscurity of north London suburbia.

From the age of three until her death at the age of 68 in 1971, she lived at 1 Avondale Road, where a plaque marks her time in this modest, red-brick end-of-terrace house. She moved here from Hull with her mother, two sisters and beloved Aunt Margaret when her father joined the Merchant Navy after his business collapsed. It was a 'house of female habitation', that she shared with her aunt after her mother died in 1919. Three years in a Kent sanatorium offered little formal education before she was nine. She did not excel academically, missed university, and from 1922 was a secretary in publishing, where the work was boring and unrewarding, but offered time to read and write.

Novel on Yellow Paper (1937) was an instant success. Two other novels followed, and in 1937 her first volume of poetry appeared. But in the 1940s and early 1950s Smith's work was unfashionable, and publication elusive. She grew isolated, bored and unhappy. In 1953 she attempted to slash her wrists. She retired on a modest pension and took up reviewing. However, *Not Waving but Drowning* (1957) saw her re-emerge, and, with *The Frog Prince* (1966), her reputation grew. She gained honours, such as the Queen's Gold Medal for Poetry in 1969. After her aunt's death in 1968, she lived out the rest of her life alone in Avondale Avenue.

Emotionally vulnerable, she also showed warmth and gaiety, and had a deep Christian faith. Perhaps significantly, she said writing novels drew her into dangerous psychic depths; with poetry she could invent characters and stories.

Address The Triangle, Palmers Green, N13 4PN | **Getting there** Train to Palmers Green | **Hours** Unrestricted | **Tip** Delightful 500-acre Broomfield Park was once a royal hunting ground, but today comprises playing fields, woods, formal gardens, lakes and ponds, and a crazy golf course (www.friendsofbroomfieldpark.org).

The pleasures of friendship are exquisite.
How pleasant to go to a friend on a visit!
I go to my friend, we walk on the grass,
And the hours and moments like minutes pass.
Stevie Smith

64 Parkway

A tale of two Bennetts

Palmers, opened in 1918 as a pet shop, is now a Grade II-listed café in Parkway, Camden Town, and merited significant mentions by two of Britain's leading writers. It is also associated with two people called Bennett, one real, the other fictional.

The real and best-known Bennett – the playwright Alan – reported in 1971 that Miss Shepherd, his lady in the van, in his short book of that title, had seen a 'long, gray snake, a boa constrictor', which looked poisonous, in Parkway. Bennett writes, 'It was keeping close to the wall and seemed to know its way and it looked as if it was heading for the van'. The eccentric Miss Shepherd, who lived in her camper van parked outside (and later in the garden of) Bennett's house nearby, told him, 'I thought I had better tell you, just to be on the safe side. I've had some close shaves with snakes'. But he dismissed what he called the 'serpent-sightings' as 'just another of Miss S's not infrequent visions'. But it may have been true for the shop had had a break-in the previous night.

The third novel from Graham Greene (see ch. 21), *It's a Battlefield* (1934), introduced the fictional Bennett, a Communist, lodging in a flat above the shop. Greene calls it a 'zoological shop', where dogs bark at each other, and when 'the traffic was almost stilled, it was possible to hear the lions roaring in [nearby] Regent's Park [zoo] to be fed'.

When the artist Paul Hogarth visited Camden Town in the 1980s for his book, *Graham Greene Country*, he found Palmer's still a pet shop but also that Parkway was 'proud of its niche in Greene country and still looks its seedy best', as in a Greene novel.

Times have changed in trendy Parkway, but signs above the original windows for 'monkeys' and 'talking parrots', as well as 'Palmers [sic]' and 'Regent's Pets' speak of past times, even if it's a cup of coffee that visitors buy today.

Address Gail's, 35-37 Parkway, NW1 7PN, +44 (0)207 267 8631, www.gailsbread.co.uk | **Getting there** Underground to Camden Town (Northern line) | **Hours** See website for opening times | **Tip** A strikingly realistic bronze statue of the singer Amy Winehouse in Stables Market on Chalk Farm Road has her in a characteristic short skirt, bouffant hairstyle, and a Star of David around her neck. She died aged 27 from alcohol poisoning in nearby Camden Square.

65 Peckham Rye

Where William Blake saw angels

The poet, artist and visionary William Blake was a lonely, solitary child, given to walking both London's streets and the countryside, which was accessible not far from his London home in Soho, where he was born at 28 Broad Street. There was nothing bucolic about the London where he often wandered: poor housing, overcrowding, workhouses, and the stench from ancient soil in ill-kept graveyards. Away from the capital, his tendency was to walk towards the south: he walked to Dulwich, Croydon and Camberwell, which at that time were only villages, and often wrote down what he saw.

As an adult, Blake is associated with visions, often expressed in his art and poetry, but as a child aged eight or nine, in around 1766, as he later related, he saw his 'first vision' on the open land of Peckham Rye. He recounted looking up and seeing a 'tree filled with angels, bright angelic wings bespangling every bough like stars'. When he returned home and told his parents of this celestial happening, only his mother's intervention stopped his father delivering a severe thrashing for apparent lies. Whether this was actually his first vision is uncertain, for his mother had beaten him for claiming to see the Prophet Ezekiel under a tree in the fields, and he claimed he saw God 'put his head to the window' when he was only four years old. Blake was not only precocious in seeing visions: at 14 he kept a sketchbook, and was also writing poems, which one biographer describes as possessing 'extraordinary fluency'.

Visions were to form a large part of Blake's writing for the rest of his life. The vision at Peckham Rye was commemorated at nearby Goose Green in 1993, a mural commissioned for the Dulwich Festival of that year, while in 2011 the Peckham artist John Hartley replanted Blake's famous angel oak on the adjourning Peckham Common, using a rescued oak sapling.

Address 34 Straker's Road, SE15 3UA, +44 (0)208 299 0861, www.peckhamryepark.org | **Getting there** Train or Overground to Peckham Rye or Honor Oak or train to East Dulwich | **Hours** Open at 7.30am but closing times vary through the year; check website for current information on visiting | **Tip** An unusual plaque to the footballer Rio Ferdinand, who lived on the Friary Estate, can be found at Leyton Square, Peckham Park Road, SE15 6TP. The plaque was erected by Southwark Council, and says it was 'voted by the people'.

66 Pemberton Gardens

Home of a nobody for the Pooters

This modest Victorian villa has been identified as 'The Laurels', Brickfield Terrace, which George and Weedon Grossmith, in their superb comedy of Victorian suburban life, made the home of the middle class, snobbish, socially aspiring Charles Pooter, narrator of their classic *Diary of a Nobody*, his 'dear wife Carrie', and their adult son Lupin. When not working in the City as a clerk, Pooter liked to be at home, for 'what good's a home, if you are never in it? "Home, Sweet Home", that's my motto,' he would say.

The couple's friends, the tiresome Cumming and Gowing, arrive by the side entrance. This is to save the servant going to the front door, thereby distracting her from her work. Pooter describes the house as having six bedrooms, a basement and a front breakfast parlour, a small front garden, and steps to the front door. It is at The Laurels where the self-important Pooter records his numerous humiliations in his diary. Poor Madeira-drinking Pooter would be horrified to know that his name has lent itself to the adjective 'Pooterish' – the tendency to believe that one's importance or influence is greater than it is.

George Grossmith was several geographical steps above his character, for he and his brother wrote the book at George's handsome house at 28 Dorset Square. First published in instalments in *Punch* in 1888-9, it became a book in 1892. Unlike Pooter, George was more adventurous in his career: both as an actor, one of the most popular entertainers of his time, and for the D'Oyly Carte Company's Gilbert and Sullivan operettas, such as *The Mikado*, *Iolanthe*, and *Yeoman of the Guard.* He also toured the UK and the USA in the 1890s with his one-man shows. Weedon, too, appeared in D'Oyly Carte operettas, and wrote novels and plays. He is also remembered for his 33 black and white line drawings for *Nobody*, which illustrate the book today.

Address 1 Pemberton Gardens, N16 5RR | Getting there Overground to Upper Holloway or Underground to Archway (Northern line) | Hours Viewable from outside only | Tip The Gothic Revival, Grade I-listed mid 19th-century Union Chapel on Compton Terrace is a church, and entertainment and drop-in centre. Take the short journey by Underground to Highbury & Islington (Victoria line).

67 The Pembroke

Armistead Maupin's leather bar local

Babycakes, the fourth in Armistead Maupin's *Tales in the City* novels, opens not in Mrs Madrigal's beloved boarding house in San Francisco's Barbary Lane, or in the gay community. Instead, it begins with the Queen, accompanied by Prince Philip. She is visiting the city on her 1983 state visit to the US, feeling a sniffle, wondering where they will dine that evening, and concerned for an upset stomach when at sea.

Moored off the coast, the royal yacht *Britannia* is missing an officer. When Michael 'Mouse' Tolliver, a bereaved resident of Mrs Madrigal, does a house exchange with the abscondee, Simon, he finds himself in a down-at-heel flat: the fictional 40 Colville Crescent in the then downmarket Notting Hill.

Mouse's local in Earl's Court is The Colehern (now The Pembroke) pub, then one of the best-known gay pubs, whose clientele included Freddie Mercury, Derek Jarman and Rudolf Nureyev. Maupin knew the pub, a leather bar, when he also lived in London in a scruffy flat. Before that, in the 1950s, The Colehern attracted a bohemian crowd, and hosted drag acts. By the standards of San Francisco, Mouse finds the pub tame, and he is not impressed. But there he meets the improbably named Wilfred, who is gay, handsome, and mixed-race. Mouse is surprised to find that Wilfred lives with his violent, drunken father two floors above his flat. Wilfred accompanies Mouse to an aristocratic country house in Gloucestershire in search of his long-lost friend Mona, daughter of Mrs Madrigal – 'Babycakes' is his affectionate term for his favoured female friends.

At the time *Babycakes* is set, AIDS is in its earliest days – Wilfred has never heard of it – but it causes the death of Jon Fielding, Mouse's lover. Swapping between London and San Francisco, even though the coming of AIDS signals the end of an era, Maupin contrives several happy endings with characteristic skill.

Address 261 Old Brompton Road, Earls Court, SW5 9JA, +44 (0)207 373 8337, www.thepembrokesw5.co.uk | **Getting there** Overground or Underground to West Brompton (District line) | **Hours** See website for current opening hours | **Tip** Travel north on the District line to Notting Hill to find The Bottle Kiln on Walmer Road. Named because of its shape, it's a 19th-century kiln that fired bricks and tiles from the area's heavy clay, which helped the development of Notting Hill.

68_Poets' Corner

Trollope's warden contemplates quandary

Poets' Corner, in Westminster Abbey, memorialises some of Britain's greatest writers, but this was no compensation to Trollope's Rev Septimus Harding in *The Warden*, the first volume of the six-novel *Barchester Chronicles* sequence, published in 1855. The conscientious, retiring, music-loving Harding, precentor of Barchester Cathedral and warden of Hiram's House alms house, is afflicted by public and domestic conflicts that mark the novels. He becomes the subject of a campaign by John Bold, a zealous young reformer, which casts aspersions on how Harding manages the charity's income. Bold initiates a law suit, but Archdeacon Grantly advises Harding, his ageing father-in-law, to stand his ground. As a result of press coverage stimulated by Bold, Harding is seen as selfish and derelict in his duties.

The clergyman travels to spend 'a long day' in London to think about resigning his post, despite the advice of his bishop and his family, and even though he knows this will plunge him into poverty. After booking into the Chapter House Coffee House near St Paul's Cathedral, he travels by omnibus to the abbey, 'determined to take sanctuary'. There, he pays tuppence to enter as a sightseer. ('Again, what a change!' comments Trollope in a footnote).

The advice he has refused and the consequences of his proposed action cause Harding to first sit for 20 minutes on a stone step, gazing at the 33-foot white marble statue of William Pitt the Elder, twice Prime Minister. A verger, seeing that he is a clergyman, says he may take a seat in the choir. He spends two hours in contemplation, walking up and down the nave and aisles of the abbey, paying no heed to the 'reverential stares' of the vergers. His decision to resign has professional consequences for him; for the life of the alms house; and the romantic life of Eleanor, his unmarried younger daughter.

Address Westminster Abbey, SW1P 3PA, +44 (0)207 222 5152, www.westminster-abbey.org | **Getting there** Underground to St James Park (District and Circle lines) or Westminster (District, Circle and Jubilee lines) | **Hours** See website for current information on visiting | **Tip** For another, architecturally very different ecclesiastical building, walk to the bottom of Victoria Street to the Catholic Westminster Cathedral, built in the Neo-Byzantine style and consecrated in 1910.

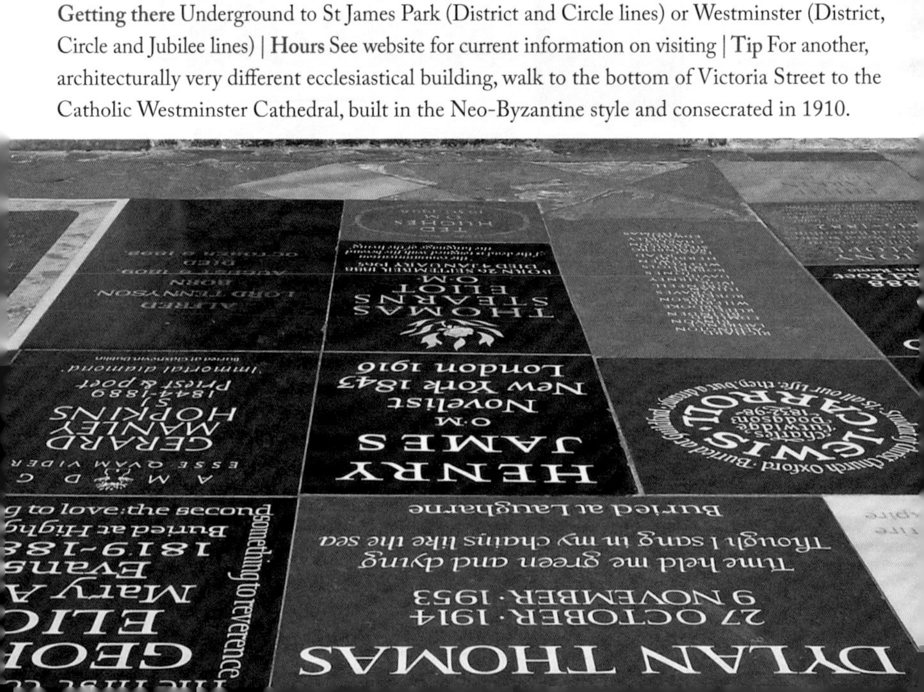

69 Pole Hill

Lawrence of Chingford

It's a far cry from the deserts of the First World War, where T. E. Lawrence made his name and created his enduring myth when he led the Arab Revolt, to the 18 acres of land at Pole Hill, Chingford. On one of the highest points of Epping Forest, he bought small parcels of land after the war. His aim was to set up a press with Vyvyan Richards, a university friend from Jesus College, Cambridge, to print fine-edition books. Richards testified to the inspiration Lawrence found in William Morris' own enthusiasm for medievalism and craftsmanship.

The two men also planned to build a medieval-style timber hall. Richards wrote, 'I have already spoken of the old timbers that he [Lawrence] rescued from a hall which our college was pulling down ... We planned to build ourselves such a hall and crown it with these carved oak king-posts and their rafters and purlins.'

However, a hut burned down in 1921 which was later replaced with a wooden building with a small garden and plunge pool. In the construction of this the two pioneers were assisted by pupils and staff from the nearby Bancroft School, where Richards taught. Richards moved to north Wales in 1922 and Lawrence continued to envisage a dream that would never be realised. In 1930 he sold the land for £3,500 to the Conservators of Epping Forest. At the time he wrote that he was sorry to lose the Hill, 'but, as a man refused by one angel hurriedly marries the next he meets, I am in love with [his Dorset cottage] Clouds Hill'. He worked on his *Seven Pillars of Wisdom* at Pole Hill, lost the manuscript at Reading Station, rewrote it, and it was published posthumously and unabridged in 1935.

Lawrence moved to Clouds Hill hopeful that money from the land would allow him an income on which to live, but in May 1935 he died in a motorcycle accident, aged only 46. Pole Hill is now marked by an obelisk and plaque.

Address Bury Road, E4 7QL | Getting there Overground to Chingford | Hours Open 24 hours | Tip North of Pole Hill, at Yardley Hill and Yates' Meadow – two other high points with stunning views of the city – there's another unusual sight in May and over August–October, when longhorn cattle can be seen grazing.

70 The Queen's Hotel

Emile Zola in exile in south London

In 1898, Zola, France's most celebrated novelist, was living in exile in this Italianate hotel in then rural Upper Norwood. A major writer of naturalist literature, Zola had become well known with his first major novel, *Thérèse Racquin* (1867), and his sequence of 20 novels, *Les Rougon-Macquart*, published between 1871 and 1893, included three of his best known works: *Nana* (1880), *Germinal* (1885), and *La Bête Humaine* (1890). However, his literary career in his native country came to a sharp halt in 1897 with the Dreyfus Affair. This involved the French-Jewish army officer Alfred Dreyfus, who was convicted and imprisoned on Devil's Island for his part in an alleged conspiracy, stoked by antisemitism.

Zola's open letter – *J'Accuse...!* – was a fierce denunciation of the General Staff. His original conviction for criminal libel forced him into exile. The conviction was overturned on a technicality and another trial ordered, but Zola was advised by his lawyer to flee, and in his absence he was again found guilty. He stayed in two London hotels, and in rural private houses and hotels. Most of his time away was spent at the Queen's Hotel, where he stayed as M. J. Richard. He first occupied a room overlooking the garden, and then took a suite on the ground floor. Here, in the mornings, he wrote *Fécondité*, which appeared the following year, the first of his *Les Quatre Évangiles*. In the afternoons he wandered in the open country, cycled, and took photographs. At separate times his wife, Gabrielle, and his other 'wife' – as he termed her – Jeanne Rozenot, with their two children, stayed with him.

The documents that had convicted Dreyfus were found to be forged, and Zola returned to France after nearly a year in exile. He received a pardon from the government in 1899, as did Dreyfus, but died the following year as a result of carbon monoxide poisoning, his final cycle of novels incomplete.

Deuxième Année. — Numéro 87

Cinq Centimes

JEUDI 13 JANVIER 1898

Directeur
ERNEST VAUGHAN

L'AURORE

Littéraire, Artistique, Sociale

Directeur
ERNEST VAUGHAN

LES ANNONCES SONT REÇUES : 142 — Rue Montmartre — 142

J'Accuse...!

LETTRE AU PRÉSIDENT DE LA RÉPUBLIQUE

Par ÉMILE ZOLA

LETTRE A M. FÉLIX FAURE

Président de la République

Monsieur le Président,

Address 122 Church Road, SE19 2UG, +44 (0)207 653 6622, www.bestwestern.co.uk | Getting there Train to Crystal Palace | Hours 24 hours | Tip Suburban Norwood may seem a long way from the gun-toting, wise-cracking Los Angeles private eye Philip Marlowe, but just half a mile away is 110 Auckland Road, where his Chicago-born creator Raymond Chandler lived with his mother, and from where he travelled each day to Dulwich College.

71 The Reform Club

Around the world in how long?

Jules Verne regarded the Reform Club as 'an imposing edifice on Pall Mall', and it is one, along with other clubs on the same street, that he could easily have found on the grand boulevards of Paris. Founded in 1836 for radicals and Whigs who supported the Reform Act of 1832, members have included Winston Churchill (see ch. 111) and H. G. Wells (see ch. 102). It was Henry James' home for a while (see ch. 80). The weight of familiarity and history thus made it a fitting place from which Verne should decide that the great journey – in the title of his most famous novel – around the world in 80 days should begin and end. His hero, Phileas Fogg, a reserved man who is, nevertheless, 'one of the oddest and most striking members' of the club, would be accompanied by his French valet, Jean Passepartout.

Why 80 days? At a time of new railroad and steamship transportation, Verne was not the only one to ask how long it would take to go around the world by such means. It is likely that he read an article in *Le Magasin Pittoresque*, published in 1870, suggesting that 80 days by steamship was the answer – although Verne suggested the journey might take 79 or 81 days, depending on whether one went east or west. This point proves critical to Fogg's journey.

Fogg, who lives in Savile Row, precisely 576 steps from the club, makes a £20,000 wager with five other club members that he can make the journey in the predicted time. He wins the bet, but only after Passepartout points to a misunderstanding about the time difference, that they returned on a Saturday, not a Sunday.

Verne was already wealthy and famous before publication of this novel, but with a stage version it would bring him worldwide fame. Verne confessed to how much he enjoyed the book, but admitted to one regret: that while he fell for all the 'extravagant things' in which his characters engaged, he could not himself participate in them.

Address 104 Pall Mall, SW1Y 5EW, +44 (0)207 930 9374, www.reformclub.co.uk | **Getting there** Underground to Green Park (Piccadilly, Jubilee and Victoria lines) or Piccadilly Circus (Piccadilly and Bakerloo lines) | **Hours** Open to members only Mon–Fri 7am–11pm, but tours may be booked via website | **Tip** The Institute of Contemporary Arts has been in the classical Carlton House Terrace since 1968. It contains a bookshop, cinema, art gallery, auditorium, and restaurant, and offers lectures, exhibitions and films (www.ica.art).

72 Robert Fitzroy Academy

D. H. Lawrence, the novel teacher

It was when the then beardless D. H. Lawrence was living in Croydon that his first novel, *The White Peacock*, was published in 1911. A qualified teacher (between 1902 and 1906 he acted as a pupil-teacher in his native Eastwood), he took a teaching job at what was then Davidson Road School – now the Robert Fitzroy Academy. He was paid £95 a year to teach 45 boys. Lawrence was a progressive and innovative teacher: he encouraged his pupils to perform Shakespeare's plays rather than read them, for example. Although he was never satisfied with his teaching abilities, his head teacher did not agree. While teaching, Lawrence lodged at nearby 12 Colworth Road from October 1908 to September 1911, then at No.16 from September to December 1911, and for the first six days of 1912.

Sons and Lovers, begun in Croydon, was published in 1913, and proved to be his literary breakthrough. During this time he also published essays, wrote two plays and read modern literature. While Lawrence felt isolated in Croydon, found teaching's administration tedious and was frustrated by his pupils, he enjoyed romantic attachments, and also met people significant in his literary life, such as the novelist Ford Maddox Heuffer (later Ford), who published his poetry, and the literary editor Edward Garnett. But double pneumonia, of which he nearly died, effectively ended his teaching career in 1911.

In March 1912, Lawrence met and fell in love with Freida von Richthofen – six years his senior, and the wife of his old professor in Nottingham. When Freida divorced, the couple married in Germany in 1914. He became a full-time writer, and following a year in Cornwall the couple lived in Germany, Italy and other parts of the world, as well as returning to England occasionally. Lawrence is commemorated by a bust in the school where he once taught, while a plaque marks both of his former homes.

Address 80 Brampton Road, Croydon, CR0 6JN, +44 (0)208 662 9700, www.robertfitzroyacademy.com | Getting there Train to East Croydon, then bus 410 to Brampton Road | Hours The bust can be viewed by emailing ask@robertfitzroyacademy.com | Tip Return to the attractive 19th-century Croydon Clock Tower in Croydon town centre for the David Lean, a small, intimate, art house-style cinema, run by volunteers (www.davidleancinema.org.uk).

73 Rose Street

Rebellious writer attacked

In this narrow passageway, then called Rose Alley, next to the Lamb and Flag public house, the poet and playwright John Dryden was attacked by thugs on 18 December, 1679. The reason for the assault is clear, but whether he was the rightful target is not. The attack was prompted by the poetic lampoon, *An Essay upon Satire*, which crudely vilified prominent individuals, including Charles II, his mistresses, and John Wilmot, the second Earl of Rochester, who was most likely behind the attack.

While some made Dryden the author, others pointed to his patron and poetic collaborator, the Earl of Mulgrave. One critic suggests that the 'stylistic banality' of the poem makes Dryden an unlikely author. Also, given that Dryden was a professional writer of such standing that he was Poet Laureate, such a satire would have affected both his standard of living and reputation. It's possible that Mulgrave was the author, while Dryden contributed to improving the text.

Since the Restoration of the monarchy in 1660, which Dryden had welcomed, he published several poems extravagantly praising the king. These were attempts to curry favour with the new regime and promote his literary career. While the king would have appointed him laureate, Rochester was no friend. Himself a poet and courtier, his satires, *An Allusion to Horace* and *The Medal of John Bayes*, which he published anonymously, have Dryden as a libertine, boasting obscenely to boost that image; but this behaviour was out of character, and the only sexual scandal that impugned his reputation was that Dryden had a mistress. A character otherwise unblemished was unusual around many of the circle with which he mixed at the time.

The location of the attack was appropriate: the pub, then the Cooper's Arms, was at one time nick-named 'The Bucket of Blood' due to bare-knuckle boxing bouts that took place in an upper room.

Address Lamb and Flag, 33 Rose Street, WC2E 9EB, +44 (0)207 497 9504, www.lambandflagcoventgarden.co.uk | Getting there Underground to Covent Garden (Piccadilly line) | Hours Alley accessible 24 hours | Tip In the Piazza, the London Transport Museum illustrates 200 years of the capital and its transport through vehicles, maps, drawings and photographs.

74_Royal Horseguards Hotel

The library without books

What was and still is called the Gladstone Library is unique – it has no books. The library had 35,000 books and over 30,000 pamphlets in what was to be Britain's largest library of 17th to 20th-century political literature. Once part of the adjoining National Liberal Club, in the 1960s and 1970s the club was in poor shape: it needed repairs, it was losing money, and its membership was declining. Liberal leader Jeremy Thorpe appointed a Canadian confidence trickster, George Marks, to staunch the financial flow. Marks, who called himself George de Chabris, claimed to be an aristocrat and multi-millionaire (he was neither), who said he would subsidise the club (he didn't).

He managed the club for nine months, during which time he defrauded the club, moved in his family rent-free, ran several dubious businesses, bought a sports car, and had the club pay his children's school fees. Claiming that the club could no longer afford a librarian, in 1977 he sold the library to Bristol University for £40,000 – a price judged to be derisory. After his dismissal, Marks agreed to pay back £60,000, a less part of what he had gained.

Later measures gave the club financial stability and a secure future. These included selling the second-floor and basement function rooms, and the 140 bedrooms from the third floor to the eighth floor, which included the Gladstone Library, to the adjoining Royal Horseguards Hotel. As a homage to the library's former existence, its empty shelves are now filled with fake book spines, resplendent in green, gold, and red.

The library has had its glory days: as recently as 1999 it played host to the lunch for the W. H. Smith Book Awards, when Beryl Bainbridge gained £10,000 prize money for her novel, *Master Georgie*. The club now operates a much smaller library acquired long after the Gladstone Library's books made their way to the West Country.

Address 2 Whitehall Court, SW1A 2EJ, +44 (0)207 523 5062, www.guoman.com | **Getting there** Underground to Embankment (Northern, Bakerloo, District, and Circle lines) or Charing Cross (Northern and Bakerloo lines) | **Hours** Contact reception to see the library | **Tip** You don't have to go to Calais to see one of Rodin's most famous works. A short walk south is Victoria Tower Gardens, next to the Houses of Parliament, where his *Burghers of Calais* stands. The sculpture was made in 1889, and commemorates the heroic end of the siege of Calais in 1347.

75 Royal Observatory

A terrorist plot in Greenwich

If art reflects life, it does so no better than in what is widely regarded as Joseph Conrad's best novel, *The Secret Agent,* in which a bomber dies when attempting to blow up the Royal Observatory in Greenwich Park. It is one of the most famous terrorist plots in fiction. This was Conrad's tenth book, and in an author's note, published in 1907, he says that he partly got the idea when discussing anarchism with a friend – likely his fellow novelist Ford Maddox Ford. One of them mentioned a failed attempt to blow up the Observatory that took place in February 1899, when the bomber in question, Martial Bourdin, blew himself up. It was, wrote the author, 'a bloodstained inanity of so fatuous a kind that it was impossible to fathom its origins by any reasonable or even unreasonable process of thought.' The friend said that the plotter was an idiot whose sister committed suicide afterwards, which gave Conrad more food for his novel.

Conrad said that he was also helped by a book of reminiscences by an Assistant Police Commissioner, in which was reproduced an exchange between the author and Sir William Harcourt, the then Home Secretary, after some unexpected anarchist outrage. The minister said: 'All that's very well. But your idea of secrecy seems to consist of keeping the Home Secretary in the dark.'

Originally conceived as a short story, the novel describes a police investigation, and paints a gloomy picture of London and anarchist circles. Adolf Verloc, a seedy shopkeeper employed by a foreign embassy to spy on revolutionary groups, is a member of these circles, and induced to instigate a bombing. Verloc persuades Stevie, his brother-in-law, who has learning difficulties, to attempt to blow up the Observatory, during which attempt the bomb explodes and kills Stevie. In her outrage against Verloc's actions, his wife, Minnie, murders him then drowns herself.

Address Blackheath Road, SE10 8XJ, +44 (0)20 8312 6608, www.rmg.co.uk | Getting there DLR to Greenwich or Cutty Sark, or train to Maze Hill | Hours Daily 10am–5pm; see website for details of bookings | Tip Board the Cutty Sark, which has 11 miles of rigging and is the world's last surviving tea clipper (www.rmg.co.uk/cutty-sark).

76_Russell Square

Where T. S. Eliot, the poet, discovered poets

In what is now part of the University of London's Birkbeck College's School of Social Science, History and Philosophy, 25 Russell Square was once the offices of Faber & Faber, where T. S. Eliot worked as a publisher for 40 years. By the time he joined in 1925, the American, who later became a British citizen and was awarded the Order of Merit and the Nobel Prize for Literature, had published *The Waste Land.*

He had taught at Harvard, arrived in England in 1914, made an unhappy first marriage to Vivienne Haigh-Wood, and tried teaching and banking. Virginia Woolf called him a 'corpse', with a 'great yellow bronze mask for a face'. He must have been unaware of this, as a photograph of her was on his office mantelpiece. Despite Woolf's description, he was said to light fire crackers in office waste bins to mark 4 July.

It was at Faber that he discovered a gift as a playwright and also converted to High Anglicanism. He enjoyed the conviviality of editorial life at Faber, which functioned like a club. He was responsible for publishing many modern poets, including Louis MacNeice, Stephen Spender, W. H. Auden, and Ted Hughes (see ch. 85). One visitor was his fellow poet George Barker, who remembered Eliot in 1939, as war clouds gathered over Europe, looking out of the window and saying in a tired voice, 'We have so very little time...'.

It was also here that Eliot met Valerie Fletcher, his secretary, whom he would marry in 1957. Thirty-eight years his junior, she would become his editor and protective literary executor. Before then, often to escape his first marriage, he would sometimes sleep in a top-floor flat. Eventually committed to an asylum, Vivienne would sometimes turn up at the office unannounced. Eliot's secretary would detain her, while he made his exit. Despite his increasing fame, Eliot remained with the company until he died in 1965.

Address 25 Russell Square, WC1B 5DT | **Getting there** Underground to Russell Square (Piccadilly line) | **Hours** Viewable from outside only | **Tip** In nearby Cartwright Gardens is a statue of the man after whom it is named: John Cartwright, the first English writer to openly maintain the independence of the USA, and who also supported universal suffrage, annual parliaments, and voting by ballot.

77_Sambourne House

Here humour and aesthetics combine

One of the lesser-known museums in London is a rare example of a house museum. For 36 years from 1875, 18 Stafford Terrace was the home of the illustrator Edward Linley Sambourne, chief cartoonist of the humorous magazine *Punch*. He lived there with his wife Marion, their two children, Roy and Maud, and their live-in servants. The house was conveniently near Marion's parents, but he was particularly attracted to other artists living nearby, making up the artistic community of Holland Park Circle. Their nine striking Victorian studio houses were designed by architects such as Norman Shaw and Philip Webb. All but two of these houses survive.

This house, on five floors but with rooms smaller than one might expect, not only shows the lives of people of the Sambournes' class of the time, but combines the contemporary aesthetic style with the Sambournes' personal tastes. It remains very much as the family created it. This is not surprising, because before becoming a museum, it was lived in by their son Roy and granddaughter Anne, who respected what had been created.

One of the first jobs the Sambournes undertook after moving in was to decorate the house in fashionable Morris & Co. wallpaper, designed by the artist and writer William Morris. Perhaps not unusually for an artist's home, an inventory of 1877 showed, among other things, over 50 vases, 70 chairs and around 700 framed prints, drawings and photographs. The walls are still generously hung with pictures and the rooms heavy with ornaments. Many are Sambourne's own cartoons and drawings for *Punch* and elsewhere. What is now Sambourne's studio was once the children's night nursery, which became the studio in 1899. Before then he had worked in the morning room and then the drawing room. Visitors can observe his work throughout the house and walk into what he called 'my own snug room'.

Address 18 Stafford Terrace, W8 7BH, +44 (0)208 994 1019, www.rbkc.gov.uk | Getting there Underground to Kensington High Street (District and Circle lines) | Hours Wed–Sun 10am–5.30pm | Tip Around the corner at 12 Holland Park Road is the much grander house of the painter Frederick (Lord) Leighton, a member of the Holland Park Circle. His work and the tiled walls make for a memorable visit (www.rbkc.gov.uk/museums).

78 The Senate House

Where 'ignorance is strength' in Newspeak

In August 1941 George Orwell became a producer with the BBC's Far Eastern section, a position he held until November 1943. In 1949, in his dystopian novel *Nineteen Eighty-Four*, Orwell placed the cabbage-smelling underground BBC canteen in his Ministry of Truth. The ministry's architectural model is not the BBC's headquarters in Portland Place, however, but the University of London's towering Senate House. In the novel he describes this as 'an enormous pyramidal structure of glittering white concrete, with 3,000 rooms, soaring up, terrace after terrace, 300 metres in the air'. On its white facade he displayed the three-decker slogans of the party: 'War is peace/Freedom is slavery/Ignorance is strength'. The ministry is, with the ministries of Love, Truth and Plenty, one of four in Oceania, ruled by the Party and Big Brother, one of the world's three power blocs, who are perpetually at war with each other.

Blue-uniformed party members produce not propaganda for the proles, the uneducated under-class, but deadening 'rubbishy newspapers containing almost nothing but sport, crime and astrology; sensational five-cent novelettes, films oozing with sex, and sentimental songs composed entirely by mechanical means'. A secret dissident worker, Winston Smith writes, erases and changes past newspaper reports and statements to show that Big Brother and the Party have always been consistent. In so doing, he helps to alter – and in some cases erase – the past, in his works in the records department.

Orwell's *Animal Farm* is an attack on the Soviet Union, but *Nineteen Eighty-Four* warns against totalitarian tendencies anywhere. In days of disinformation, 'fake news' and electronic surveillance – citizens of Oceania have 'telescreens' in their homes and workplaces that monitor their actions and movements – Orwell's warnings may not seem so far-fetched as they did when the novel was first published.

Address Malet Street, WC1E 7HU, +44 (0)207 862 8500, www.senate.ac.uk | Getting there Underground to Russell Square (Piccadilly line) | Hours Daily 7am–7pm | Tip Senate House again became an emblem of dictatorship, when in 1985 it served as the headquarters of Ian McKellen's 1930s British fascist dictator, in a modern dress cinema version of *Richard III* – and a very good movie it is too!

79 The Sherlock Holmes

Have a pint with the Great Detective

This pub was the Northumberland Hotel, where Sir Henry Baskerville, heir to the Baskerville title, estate and fortune, stayed when coming from Canada in what is one of Arthur Conan Doyle's most famous Sherlock Holmes detective novels. Here, Sir Henry met Holmes and his assistant Dr Watson to be told of the legend of the savage hound of the Baskervilles, believed responsible for the recent death of Sir Henry's uncle, Sir Charles Baskerville.

The rest of the novel takes place in the Baskerville county of Devon, but it is appropriate that the Sherlock Holmes Pub commemorates the great detective other than by its name, for upstairs is the kind of place where Holmes would have contemplated his deductions. The fearsome hound's stuffed head adorns the walls, and the stairway is lined with even more intriguing Holmesiana: numerous stills from various Sherlock Holmes films and plays, as well as theatrical posters – and, of course, photographs of Conan Doyle himself. This leads to the first floor, where in the corner of a dining room is a glass-walled reproduction of the detective's study, as it would have been in his Baker Street residence.

The study has a life-sized manikin of Holmes in his dressing gown, as he stands next to a chair on which rest a violin, a decanter, and a copy of the *Daily Telegraph*. There is a desk strewn with papers (along with a print of Charles Dickens), photographs and pictures, and a heavy Victorian fireplace and mantelpiece with a mirror above. In one corner is Holmes' chemical collection.

The items were part of an exhibition mounted in 1951 for the Festival of Britain. After the exhibition returned from New York, where it caused great interest, many of the items went to the pub to create the study. Although far less well-known than the Sherlock Holmes Museum on Baker Street, this exhibition pre-dates it by nearly 40 years.

Address 10 Northumberland Street, WC2N 5DB, +44 (0)207 930 2644, www.greeneking-pubs.co.uk | **Getting there** Underground to Embankment (Northern, Bakerloo, District and Circle lines) or train or Underground to Charing Cross (Jubilee and Northern lines) | **Hours** See website for current information on visiting | **Tip** Nearby 36 Craven Street is the only surviving home of Benjamin Franklin, one of the founding fathers of the USA. Now a house museum, the rooms are sparsely furnished but used for events and exhibitions.

80 Sir John Soane's Museum

Henry James visits inspirational antiquities

Sir John Soane's Museum is a collection of thousands of objects, from Egyptian antiquities and Roman sculpture to models and plans of then contemporary buildings. After the novelist Henry James visited Sir John Soane's Museum he featured it in *A London Life* (1888).

James' Laura Wing, a young American in London, takes a hansom cab to Lincoln's Inn Fields, finding herself dissatisfied with St Paul's Cathedral. She visits the museum with a compatriot and suitor, Mr Wendover. The museum appeals to Wing, as the year before she had visited 'the curiosities, the antiquities, the monuments' and found 'old corners of history' and 'houses in which great men had lived and died'. She finds it 'one of the most curious things in London and one of the least known'. James describes it as 'a fine old dwelling house'. In fact, Soane had created one building from three by the time he died in 1837.

A storm threatens and the sky darkens as Laura and Wendover arrive, and Wendover relates that inside 'the place gives one the impression of a sort of Saturday afternoon of one's youth – a long, rummaging visit, under indulgent care, to some eccentric and rather alarming old, travelled person,' and that 'it would be a very good place to find a thing you couldn't find anywhere else – it illustrated the prudent virtue of keeping.'

A staff member guides them to the basement as the storm reaches its height. Here vaults are dim, walls encrusted, and there are passages and nooks and crannies. They view 'strange vague things … some of which had a wicked, startling look … like a cave of idols'. Laura grows frightened when a flash of lightning illuminates one, then two figures in the shadows, accompanied by a shriek. It is her married sister, Selina, on an illicit assignation with her lover, in a place as empty and obscure as they could have found anywhere in the city.

Address 13 Lincoln's Inn Fields, WC2A 3BP, +44 (0)207 405 2107, www.soane.org | Getting there Underground to Holborn (Central line) | Hours Free entry Wed–Sun 10am–5pm and bank holidays | Tip For those with a strong stomach, the fascinating Hunterian Museum within the Royal College of Surgeons, with its anatomy and pathology collections, is on the opposite side of Lincoln's Inn Fields (www.rcseng.ac.uk).

81 St Andrew Undershaft

London commemorates a Londoner

Nothing would have pleased John Stowe more than that, as someone who lived his whole life in the city he chronicled, he would be commemorated by a statue in St Andrew's Undershaft. Built in 1532, the church is a short distance from where he was born, was a parishioner, and was buried following his death in 1605, at the age of 80. The memorial, in marble and plaster, and commissioned by his wife, shows him standing at his desk writing a manuscript.

His *Survey of London*, published in 1598, is a ward-by-ward topographical and historical tour of the City of London, and a unique account of its buildings, social conditions, customs and history. He worked as a tailor for 30 years after an apprenticeship. During that time he developed an interest in antiquarianism and began writing various publications, not least an expanded edition of Chaucer's poems.

The word 'survey' is misleading in overlooking his gift for anecdote, which enlivens the book and its strong narrative. Living and social conditions as well as prices give a unique view of late-Elizabethan urban life. Small as the city was then, Stowe made his visits, from churches to alleyways, on foot, which entailed, as he himself complained, 'many a weary mile ... many a cold winter's night's study'. Such testimony speaks of the extensive on-the-spot research he undertook. The book was added to within a few years when it was reissued and expanded. This process continued with later editions, and it remains in print over 400 years later.

But Stowe's body no longer rests beneath his memorial. 'The ancient dead', he reported, were often removed from their burial places to make room for others. In 1732 his grave 'was spoiled of his injured remains by certain men'. Where he now rests is not known, but each year the Lord Mayor of London and City officials attend a ceremony, and place a quill pen in Stow's hand.

Address St Mary Axe, EC3A 3BB, +44 (0)207 283 2231, www.st-helens.org.uk | Getting there DLR or Underground to Bank (Northern and Central lines) or Overground or Underground to Liverpool Street (Elizabeth, Hammersmith & City, Central, District and Circle lines) | Hours Daily 9am–5pm, but see website for services | Tip Bevis Marks Synagogue (see ch. 82), built in 1701, is the oldest in Britain and the only one in Europe in continuous use for 300 years; its beautiful interior is not to be missed (www.sephardi.org.uk).

82 St Andrew's Church

Novelist Jew becomes Christian prime minister

Had a Jewish scholar not had a dispute with his family's synagogue, Bevis Marks, Benjamin Disraeli would not have been Britain's first (and so far, only) Jewish prime minister. And even more unusual: a prime minister who was also a novelist. While father Isaac, a scholar and writer, paid his annual synagogue dues, he rarely attended, and when the synagogue appointed him to serve as a parnass or warden, he politely refused. This was partly on theological grounds, and partly to avoid being distracted from his intellectual pursuits. When the governing body imposed a fine of £40, he refused to pay and sent them a violent letter.

In 1804, when Disraeli was born, Jews could not be members of Parliament – a bar not lifted until 1858. When Isaac's far more devout father, the elder Benjamin, died at the age of 90 in 1813, the family's frail hold on active Judaism was severed, and enabled Isaac to give up membership of Bevis Marks. Isaac was now neither Jew nor Christian, but would have been aware that much would be denied his children, especially his sons, if they were not members of the Anglican Church (Catholics, like Jews, were also deprived of their civil rights). A friend's theological arguments, too, seem to have meant that in July 1817, 12-year-old Benjamin, his two brothers and his sister were all baptised in the thousand-year-old St Andrew's Church, Holborn.

Disraeli would now be free to stand for Parliament, which he did successfully in 1837. He became prime minister for 10 months in 1868, and again for six years in 1874. He completed 17 novels, one which, *Sybil* (1845) had a secondary title, *The Two Nations*, which entered the language to encapsulate the then state of Britain, but which continues to be used in political discussion. Disraeli also wrote a play and eight works of non-fiction, including biography, history and politics.

Address 5 St Andrew Street, EC4 3AF, +44 (0)20 7583 7394, www.standrewholborn.org.uk | **Getting there** Underground to Chancery Lane (Central line) | **Hours** See website for visiting and services | **Tip** Easily missed is the elaborately decorated St Sepulchre drinking fountain (Holborn Viaduct/Ely Place, EC1A 2DQ). It was the first of a philanthropic venture in 1859, when the dangers of contaminated water had become all too apparent.

83 Stationers' Hall

Literature gains its official stamp

In 1673, the New Hall was built, after Abergavenny Hall, original home of the Worshipful Company of Stationers (now 'and Newspaper Makers'), had been destroyed seven years earlier by the Great Fire of London (see ch. 1). But it took another three years for Stephen College, 'the Protestant joiner', to be employed to panel the hall. One of the oldest livery companies – they were founded to represent practitioners of ancient trades such as fishmongers, goldsmiths, fan-makers and drapers – the Stationers' Hall has the most beautiful panelling, as well as magnificent gardens.

The company was founded in 1403 when the Mayor of the City of London approved the formation of a stationers' guild, whose members were text writers and illuminators of manuscript books, booksellers, bookbinders, and suppliers of parchment, pens and paper. A stationer was one who traded from a 'stationery' stall around St Paul's Cathedral. The Royal Society was licensed to print in 1662. At one time, it was where all copyrights had to be registered, as well as, in times past, enjoying a lucrative monopoly in the production of almanacs: 400,000 copies of 30 different almanac titles were published in 1687, which ended when the market was deregulated in 1775.

It was also part of the pageantry of the City: members in scarlet and brown robes took part in festive parades, or sailed down the Thames on their ceremonial barge. Today, members still represent the older callings, but are also involved with modern visual and graphic communications industries, design and photography, book publishing, and newspapers and periodicals.

The first presentation of the Booker Prize (see ch. 36) was at the Stationer's Hall in 1969, when P. J. Newby won with *Something to Answer For*, and W. L. Webb chaired the judges, who included the writer Dame Rebecca West and poet Stephen Spender.

Address Ave Maria Lane, EC4M 7DD, +44 (0)207 446 2513, www.stationershall.co.uk | **Getting there** Train or Underground to Blackfriars (District and Circle lines) or train or Underground to St Paul's (Central line) | **Hours** Tours can be arranged by contacting sales@stationers.org | **Tip** Most people know that the Great Fire of London began in Pudding Lane near London Bridge. However, the Golden Boy of Pye Corner, a life-sized, gilded statue, at the corner of Cock Lane and Giltspur Street (EC1A 3DD), is where it was stopped. Dating from the time of the fire, the statue was gilded in the 1800s.

84 St Frideswide's Mission

Calling the midwives

What was once the St Frideswide's Mission, this large, handsome Queen Anne-style, red brick building, opened in 1893, was partly the former convent of the Anglican Order of St John the Divine, which Jennifer Worth transformed into the Order of St Raymond Nonnatus. In her autobiographical trilogy set in the 1950s and 1960s, beginning in 2002 with *Call the Midwife,* her nuns live in Nonnatus House. In actual life, clergy lived in another part of the building, now converted into apartments.

The nuns pioneered midwifery training in the 19th century, and for much of the period represented the only professional service devoted to bringing safer childbirth to the poor. As a midwife in the 1950s, Worth worked with the nuns in a large area of the East End that encompassed Limehouse, Stepney, Millwall, the Isle of Dogs, Cubitt Town, Poplar, Mile End, and Whitechapel. It was a desperately deprived area, where extended families of parents, children, cousins and grandparents lived for generations, unlikely to move more than a few – largely car-free – streets away from where they were born.

There is nothing sentimental about Jennifer Worth's books: although there are some high-paid, skilled jobs, men work largely in the docks for low pay, there is unemployment, domestic abuse, gang warfare, violence, pub brawls and prostitution. Single motherhood is stigmatised, and women work at home with none of the benefits offered by today's modern conveniences, such as dishwasher, washing machine or tumble dryer. But, Worth wrote: 'When I lived and worked there I cannot remember a door being locked, except at night.'

Worth followed her first book with two other best-sellers about the East End: *Shadows of the Workhouse* and *Farewell to the East End.* She died in May 2011, a year before *Call the Midwife* was brought to the TV screen, confirming her books' long-lived popularity.

Address Lodore Street, E14 6LY | Getting there DLR to All Saints | Hours Viewable from outside only | Tip The Ragged Museum graphically illustrates the life of the school and the destitute children who attended (www.raggedschoolmuseum.org.uk).

85 St George the Martyr

The short, unhappy marriage of two major poets

Four months after they met, Sylvia Plath and Ted Hughes, two of the most acclaimed poets of the 20th century, married on 16 June, 1956 in this early 18th-century church in the heart of Bloomsbury. It was perhaps an appropriate date for two writers, for that day is Bloomsday – a celebration of the life and work of the novelist James Joyce, and the day on which the events in his novel, *Ulysses*, occur (see ch. 14). Only Hughes' mother, Aurelia, was present at their wedding, and he was wearing his only suit; Plath's family remained in her native USA.

The couple met in Cambridge, kissed passionately and slept together at Hughes' multi-occupied flat in 18 Rugby Street near the church. She remembered spending their wedding night in a single bed at the flat amid 'the dust & grease & the carrot peels'. Despite this, he memorialised the flat in his poem '18 Rugby Street'. They honeymooned in Benidorm by way of a night in Paris, and when they returned Plath resumed her studies in Cambridge.

After a later move for a time in America, she received treatment for mental illness: she was only 21 when she made the first of several suicide attempts. Back in London in 1959, they took a flat in 3 Chalcot Square, Primrose Hill, and enjoyed the company of fellow poets such as T. S. Eliot (see ch. 76) and Stephen Spender. Hughes wrote while Plath continued her studies, and walked in Regent's Park and on Parliament Hill Fields. In 1961 they moved to Devon, where the second of their two children was born. Here, Plath discovered that Hughes was having an affair. Missing London, she left him and moved to 23 Fitzroy Road, Primrose Hill. She enjoyed the city, her poetry was published, and in January 1963 her only novel, *The Bell Jar*, came out. Tragically, however, the next month, deeply depressed, Plath made sure her children were asleep, then gassed herself to death. She was 30 years old.

Address 44 Queen Square, WC1N 3AH, +44 (0)207 404 4407, www.sgtm.org | Getting there Underground to Russell Square (Piccadilly line) | Hours See website for opening hours and service times | Tip By all means visit nearby Coram Fields – but adults must be accompanied by a child! These playing fields were once surrounded by the buildings of the Foundling Hospital, with a large internal courtyard. Look at the comparatively small building at the north end to judge how large the orphanage would have been (www.coramfields.org.uk).

86 St Leonard's Terrace

Where Dracula was conceived

While there's a blue plaque on No. 18, it was at No. 17, in 1890, that Bram Stoker began making notes for what would become *Dracula*. The Dubliner moved to this tall, narrow, attractive house in 1885. He had worked in the Dublin civil service, as a theatre critic, and from 1878 for 27 years as secretary to Sir Henry Irving, and business manager of the actor's Lyceum Theatre. But he had always hankered after a literary life. Married with a son and hard at work for Irving, he managed to publish five of his eighteen books between 1881 and 1895.

While writing these books and studying for the Bar, he was also reading about the vampire myth, eastern Europe, and dreamt of a Gothic adventure story about Englishmen pursuing a Hungarian vampire. Part of the novel was written here, as well as in Whitby, where some of the action also takes place. Much of *Dracula* is set in London: Dracula's house in Piccadilly, the London Zoo, while two vampire hunters, Dr John Steward and Dr Abraham Van Helsing, catch a cab to the city at the Spaniards Inn in Hampstead after dining nearby in Jack Straw's Castle, then a pub.

Telling the fantastical story through telegrams, letters, diary entries, newspaper cuttings, and ships' logs, with multiple narrators, Stoker creates an air of realism. He also draws on the Celtic idea of 'shape shifting': Dracula appears in human form, as a white mist, a bat and a wolf; he is old, he is young. Dracula has many interpretations, geopolitical and psychosexual among them.

In 1922, 25 years after the book's publication in 1897, and 10 years after Stoker's death, the silent German Expressionist film *Nosferatu* was the first of what would be dozens of Dracula films, which often stray well away from Stoker's book. Yet, despite the dominance of the cinema image, and while the novel appeared to a mixed reception, it is now firmly established in the pantheon of Gothic romance.

Address 17 St Leonard's Terrace, SW3 4QB | Getting there Underground to Sloane Square (District and Circle lines) | Hours Viewable from outside | Tip Many artists are associated with Chelsea but one who (literally) left his mark was Sir Jacob Epstein. Between 1909 and 1914 he worked in a studio on the site of Roper's Garden, located on nearby Old Church Street. His unfinished stone relief, unveiled in 1972, commemorates the fact.

87 St Michael's Church

Coleridge's remains found in wine cellar

In 1834, 61-year-old Samuel Taylor Coleridge, author of the epic poems *Kubla Khan* and *The Rime of the Ancient Mariner*, died and was interred in the burial ground in the high street in Highgate. However, when the new Highgate School Chapel was built in 1866, the Coleridge vault lay in the exposed undercroft of the new building, and fell into disrepair. In 1961 Coleridge's remains, along with those of his wife, Sarah, his daughter, son-in-law, and grandson, were moved to the crypt of St Michael's Church, where he had worshipped, and the consecration of which he had attended in 1832. The Poet Laureate John Masefield gave an address on the occasion.

Coleridge was now closer to his home, 'The Grove' (No. 3), where he lived for the last 16 years of his life, along with Dr James Gillman and his wife, and where he died as a 'patient/lodger'. The hope was that Dr Gillman could treat his patient's feelings of despair and isolation, and the opium addiction that he had suffered for most of his life. Coleridge warned the doctor that he would have to be 'watched carefully', but found calm and peace and again began to write.

A slate slab, which lays directly above the coffins, was set in the central aisle of the church, which included his own words, which asks 'the Christian passer-by… Child of God' to say a prayer for 'STC' that he might 'find life in death'. The crypt was, in fact, the former wine cellar of Ashhurst House, built in 1694, that had stood on the site on which the church was later built.

After 1961, the crypt was largely forgotten about. Some assumed that the Coleridge family rested in the far corner of the crypt, but in 2018, during excavations in the church, the lead coffins of the family were discovered, seen at first through a ventilation block in the bricked-up wine cellar – it transpired that Coleridge was buried below the slab in what had been the wine cellar after all.

Address South Grove, N6 6BJ, +44 (0)208 340 7279, www.stmichaelshighgate.org | Getting there Underground to Archway (Northern line) | Hours Crypt can be visited by emailing info@thecoleridgetrust.com | Tip Nearby Hampstead Heath offers almost 800 acres of woodland, playing fields, swimming ponds, and meadows of tall grass – and no fewer than 60 commemorative plaques!

88 Stoke Newington Church Street

Where Edgar Allan Poe was educated

Edgar Allan Poe had experienced an unsettled childhood by the time he sailed to the UK from his native USA in 1815, along with his foster parents, John and Frances Allan. Poe was born in Boston, one of three children of American actor, David Poe, and English-born actress, Elizabeth Poe. His father abandoned the family in 1810, the year after Poe's birth, and a year later his mother died of tuberculosis. John Allan was a successful merchant. The couple took him to the UK, and he spent a short time at school in Irvine, Ayrshire, from where Allan originated. Then, until summer 1817, he attended school in Chelsea.

Poe enjoyed his school life, and had learned to read Latin by the age of nine. The 'enchanted days' came to an end two years later, however, when he was enrolled at the Manor School, Stoke Newington Church Street, where Daniel Defoe had once lived (see ch. 26). In an autobiographical short story, *William Wilson*, author of *The Pit and the Pendulum* and *The Fall of the House of Usher*, referred to the area as 'a misty-looking village'. Under the oversight of the disciplinarian head teacher, Reverend John Bransby, Poe took dancing lessons and continued his French and Latin studies. Bransby regarded Poe as 'intelligent, wayward and wilful'; his adoptive father praised him for being a good scholar.

The family returned to the USA in 1820. Poe spent 10 months at the University of Virginia, took to journalism, served in the army, got himself discharged by purposely getting court-martialled, and wrote a number of books and short stories. Having achieved some prominence, he died at the age of 40 following a life of heavy drinking and chronic financial uncertainty – a period during which his wife also died. Today, a bust and a plaque on the building now on the site are reminders of Poe's north London schooling.

Address 172 Stoke Newington Church Street, N16 7JL | Getting there Overground to Stoke Newington | Hours Unrestricted | Tip Green Lane is home to Clissold Park, one of the least-known but most delightful London parks. Its 54 acres allow for cycling, privacy, relaxation, and places to eat, with a small zoo and a children's playground (www.clissoldpark.com).

89 St Pancras Old Church

Unusual place for a literary courtship

Mary Godwin, daughter of Mary Wollstonecraft, feminist and author, and the anarchist philosopher William Godwin, was 15 when, in November 1812, she met the poet Percy Bysshe Shelley, her parents' ardent disciple. After staying in Dundee, she was spending seven months at the home of her father and stepmother (Wollstonecraft died 11 days after Mary's birth), when Shelley came to visit the family home in Somers Town, St Pancras, with his wife Harriet. Sixteen months later she returned to live permanently in her parents' home.

In May 1814, Mary and Shelley developed a passionate relationship, and courted in the nearby ancient churchyard of St Pancras Old Church, where she was in the habit of visiting her mother's grave (the body was removed in 1851 but the tomb remains). Here, Shelley confessed his love. She later described this time as 'careless, free youth', while he saw in her 'The irresistible [*sic*] wildness & sublimity of her feelings'. She was nearly 17 and eager to write, and he was five years her senior and a published poet. They saw one another as ideal mates, and he saw his own marriage at an end, although he had a child.

Godwin expressed his opposition to Shelley, but, with a carriage waiting, Mary and Shelley, accompanied by her 15-year-old step-sister Claire Clairmont, eloped to the continent in July 1814. In Switzerland, she wrote *Frankenstein* (1818), the most famous of her seven novels. The couple returned to England when she was pregnant, in debt and facing social ostracism. She described their life together as 'very political as well as poetical'. They married in 1816, after Harriet Shelley committed suicide. They returned to Italy in 1818, where their fourth and only surviving child, Percy Florence Shelley, was born in 1819. In 1822 Shelley drowned in Italy. Mary returned to England in 1823 and died of a brain tumour in 1851.

Address Pancras Road, NW1 1UL, +44 (0)207 424 0724, stpancrasoldchurch.posp.co.uk | Getting there Underground to King's Cross (Piccadilly, Northern, Metropolitan & City and Circle lines) or train to King's Cross | Hours Daily 9.30am–3pm or 5pm; see website for services | Tip King's Cross Station is where Harry Potter began his Hogwarts journey. There is, of course, no platform 9¾, but you can see his half-disappeared luggage trolley, with two suitcases, set into the wall on the way to the real platform 9 (www.kingscross.co.uk).

90 St Paul's Cathedral

John Donne designs his own memorial

It's rare for a subject to have a hand in the design of his or her statue that is to be erected after death, but the metaphysical poet John Donne, whose subject matter ranged from sensual poems to sermons against sex and sin, Latin translations to epigrams, was no respecter of tradition. For example, a secret marriage to Ann More in 1601, 12 years his junior, produced 12 children. 14 years later he was ordained as an Anglican deacon. However, he only took holy orders because he was instructed to do so by the king. In the year of his marriage he was elected a member of parliament, and again in 1614. Although born into an old Catholic family and related to St Thomas More, he seems to have become an Anglican for reasons of social and professional advancement.

His white marble statue stands in the South Quire of St Paul's Cathedral, where, from 1621, for the last decade of his life, Donne was dean. Donne knew he was dying and asked an artist to sketch him wearing a shroud. The sketch is lost, but it served as the basis of the statue by master mason Nicholas Stone for his work of 1631-32, showing the shrouded poet rising from his funeral urn.

Donne's own epitaph is at the foot of the statue, in Latin. The statue is one of the few monuments to survive the Great Fire of London of 1666 (see ch. 1), which destroyed Old St Paul's. It is said that, during the conflagration, it fell through the floor and into the crypt, only to be discovered in one piece. Its base is scorched, a visible reminder not only of the cathedral's destruction, but also the devastation of the city itself.

There is also a bust of Donne in St Paul's Churchyard. Donne's greatest fame as a poet came after his death, as much of his work was published posthumously. A wider audience became aware of his work when his *Poems* was published in 1633. It went into six editions 23 years after his death.

IOHANNES DONNE
SAC · THEOL · PROFESS
POST VARIA STVDIA QVIBVS AB
ANNIS TENERRIMIS FIDELITER NEC
INFELICITER INCVBVIT INSTINCTV
ET IMPVLSV SPIR · SCTI MONI-
·TV ET HORTATV REGIS IAC-
·OBI ORDINES SACROS AMPLEX-
·VS ANNO SVI IESV 1614
ET SVÆ ÆTAT 42 DECANATV
HVIVS ECCLES INDVTVS 27
NOVEMB 1621 EXVTVS MORTE
VLTIMO DIE MARTII A 1631
HIC LICET IN OCCIDVO CINERE
ASPICIT EVM CVIVS NOMEN
EST ORIENS

Address Paul's Churchyard, EC4M 8AD, +44 (0)207 246 8350, www.stpauls.co.uk | Getting there Underground to St Paul's (Central line) | Hours Mon, Tue, Thu, Fri & Sat doors open 8.30am; Wed 10am; last entry 4pm; tours and talks available Mon – Sat usually between 11am and 3pm; free to sightseeing ticket holders | Tip Behind the cathedral is Temple Bar, an entrance to Paternoster Square. Until 1878 it stood at the junction of Fleet Street and The Strand. Here, the Lord Mayor of London would greet monarchs when they left royal Westminster to make an official visit to the City of London.

91_Strawberry Hill House

Gothic residence for gothic writer Horace Walpole

Horace Walpole was not only the author of *The Castle of Otranto* but, over 40 years, created a battlemented fantasy, from a couple of cottages, in an appropriate Gothic style, which he named Strawberry Hill House. With its great collection of treasures, Walpole called it 'a little Gothic castle'. He had rented one of the cottages in 1747, 17 years before his best-known work emerged from a nightmare he experienced at his house, where the book was written.

The book is the first gothic novel, published in 1764, purporting to be an authentic medieval manuscript written in 'the purest Italian' by a pseudonymous Italian priest, with a pseudonymous English translator. The effect was immediate, for publication created a great sensation, which caused Walpole, third son of Britain's first prime minister, Sir Robert Walpole, to reveal his authorship the following year. The second edition described it as a 'gothic story' – the first time that the description was used. The term itself was drawn from the idea of medieval ruins and buildings. In the book, Walpole brought in many of the elements associated with the gothic novel, such as remote castles, old buildings, tunnels, gloomy staircases, isolated shrines and battlements, as well as hidden identities, violent passions, mystery, suspense and the supernatural. The plot is ostensibly about inheritance, but that cannot hide the main theme of love – and the lack of it.

While Walpole entertained ambassadors and royalty at his home, he allowed four visitors a day for conducted tours. Strawberry Hill House itself lived up to its owner's description, for it has features such as book cases that mimic church quires, pinnacles, and a round tower. He and his friends, whom he called 'goths', would meet in the house. Ironically, perhaps, it is now part of St Mary's University College, a Catholic institution.

Address 268 Waldegrave Road, Twickenham, TW1 4ST, +44 (0)208 744 1241, www.strawberryhillhouse.org.uk | **Getting there** Train to Strawberry Hill, Overground or Underground to Richmond (District line), then R68 bus | **Hours** Sun–Wed 11am–4pm; garden and garden café: Sun–Thu 10am–4pm; tours available via +44 (0)208 744 1241 +206 | **Tip** The Eel Pie Island Museum less than a mile away offers its own brand of interest and eccentricity. Tour information via www.eelpieislandmuseum.co.uk.

92 St Thomas' Hospital

Somerset Maugham, from doctor to novelist

In 1892, at the age of 18, Somerset Maugham took one of the most fateful decisions of his life. Always wanting to live in London, he entered St Thomas' Hospital in Lambeth as a medical student. He was trained by the use of body parts bought from the local workhouse: £5 for a corpse; head and neck at 15 shillings; abdomen at seven shillings and six pence. Shy and inhibited, he was no sportsman like other male students, and particularly felt his lack of university education. While secretly bisexual, he visited prostitutes, which allowed him to join in the sexual banter of his colleagues.

Lambeth was one of the poorest districts of London, with high infant mortality rates and large families living in damp and cramped accommodation. St Thomas' offered free medical care, and Maugham came into contact with those seeking it on a daily basis, while observing the lives of local people as he walked back and forth to his lodgings in Vincent Square, Victoria. Maugham had been unsuccessful with two short stories, but from what he saw on his daily walks came an idea for his first novel, written in three months and published in 1897, the year he qualified as a doctor.

Liza of Lambeth tells of four months in the tragic life of 18-year-old Liza Kemp, a factory worker, who lives with her alcoholic mother in one room in fictional Vere Street, off the actual Westminster Bridge Road, which runs near the old hospital. The novel is determinedly realist, featuring domestic abuse, bigamy, unwanted pregnancy, miscarriage, adultery and marital tension, but Maugham also depicts Liza's longings for love, and for a world beyond the narrow confines of the one in which she lives. The novel was well received, and its first printing sold out. On the strength of his startling initial success, Maugham gave up medicine, and began his 65-year career as one of the 20th century's best known and best paid writers.

Address Westminster Bridge Road, SE1 7EH | Getting there Underground to Westminster (Jubilee, District, and Circle lines) or Lambeth North (Bakerloo line) | Hours Viewable 24 hours outside only; the best views of the extensively preserved older part of the building in Lambeth Palace Road are from Westminster or Lambeth bridges | Tip The steps at the southern end of Westminster Bridge lead to the moving National COVID Memorial. This one kilometer wall features the names of victims written in red hearts.

93_Tavistock Street

Where De Quincey got high

It was in his lodgings at 36 Tavistock Street, now a restaurant, that Thomas De Quincey wrote *Confessions of an English Opium Eater*. He recounts the pleasures and pains of his addiction to the then legal drug, which he first took to ease neuralgia when he came to London as a young man. It was here that he met the poets Samuel Coleridge, William Wordsworth (see ch. 107) and Robert Southey, and decided to devote his life to literature. When he returned in 1811, he left his wife – who bore him eight children – in Grasmere in the Lake District. In 1821, he moved to a small room at the back of 4 York Street, in what was then a far from desirable district.

Confessions appeared in book form in 1822 and soon after, the poet Thomas Hood visited to find De Quincey 'at home in a German ocean of literature, in a storm, flooding all the floor, the tables and the chairs – billows of books …'. His reputation was made, but his debts remained. De Quincey often hid from creditors, several times returning to the Lake District, yet he seems to have made this his home until at least 1825.

De Quincey's mother added the 'De' to Quincey – the blue plaque misspells it as 'de Quincy' – when his father died when De Quincey was eight. His was somewhat of a peripatetic, sickly and solitary childhood. He gained a place at Oxford at the age of 15, but pulled out after 19 months. He took to the road, mostly in Wales, but was allowed to return to Oxford when he ran out of money. He turned to journalism and essay writing. A Mancunian by birth, he later moved to Edinburgh and became a contributor to journals such as the prestigious *Blackwood's Magazine*. His *Recollections of the Lakes and the Lake Poets*, published before *Confessions*, remains a work of some importance due to his portraits of Wordsworth, Southey, Coleridge and others. He died aged of 74 in Edinburgh, where he is buried.

GREATER LONDON COUNCIL
THOMAS
de QUINCY
1785-1859
wrote
Confessions of an
English Opium Eater
in this house

Address Café Murano, 36 Tavistock Street, WC2E 7PB, +44 (0)207 240 3654, www.cafemurano.co.uk | Getting there Underground to Covent Garden (Piccadilly line) | Hours Viewable 24 hours | Tip Also in Covent Garden, the London Transport Museum details the growth of the capital over the last 200 years, with the development of all forms of public road and tube transport, from horse-drawn carriages to the electric bus; www.ltm.co.uk.

94 The Temple Church

Dark deeds, eccentric theology and medieval myth

'Everyone loves a conspiracy,' says the librarian in *The Da Vinci Code.* Few, though, would have thought – at least before Dan Brown published his book – that one would be sought in this 12th-century Gothic-Romanesque church, a hidden gem. It came to widespread public notice when Brown made use of it in his novel, and when it later featured in the film of the book, starring Tom Hanks. It is the church that the main characters, Robert Langston, Sophie Neveu and Sir Leigh Teabing, visit when trying to solve the riddle in their search for the Holy Grail: 'In London lies a knight a Pope interred / His labour's fruit a Holy wrath incurred / You seek the orb that ought be on his tomb / It speaks of Rosy flesh and seeded womb.'

But many visitors to The Temple Church will be less interested in Dan Brown than in its history and architecture, as well as the church's concerts. The Temple Church is in two parts – the eastern half is recognisable as an 'ordinary' church, with aisles and an altar, while the western part is round, with large columns ringing its central space and supporting the upper drum. This section was built in the shape of the Church of the Holy Sepulchre in Jerusalem, where Christ is said to have died and been buried, and rose from the dead, and which has been visited by millions of tourists and pilgrims.

In *The Da Vinci Code*, Langston, Neveu and Teabing are seeking an effigy on a knight's tomb without the orb that should be there. They find nine stone-engraved tombs, with effigies of knights in full armour, and the 10th under a plain gravestone. But this is no coincidence, for the two churches are linked, as to be buried in the Temple Church is to be 'buried' in the Jerusalem church. But also, with Christ's Second Coming history ends, and the dead are called to judgment. The knights await that happening, buried 'in' Jerusalem, when Christ will summon them.

Address Temple, EC4Y 7BB, +44 (0)207 353 8559, www.templechurch.com | Getting there Underground to Temple (District and Circle lines) | Hours Mon–Fri 10am–4pm; see website for Sunday services | Tip 2 Temple Place is the palatial neo-Gothic mansion of William Waldorf (1st Viscount) Astor, publisher, diplomat and property owner (he built the Waldorf Astoria Hotel in New York), and was designed as an office for his estate, with an unlimited budget. Tours available (www.twotempleplace.org).

95 Temple Tube Station

Where the author sought him and found him

Novelists gain inspiration in many different places and circumstances, but coming up with an 18th-century aristocratic adventurer while waiting for a London tube train is certainly unusual. In Paris, Baroness Orczy had conceived the idea of a play that became the 12-volume *Scarlet Pimpernel* series of novels. But it was on the westbound platform of Temple Station, as she waited to travel home to Kensington, that she came upon her idea of the 'perfect English gentleman' – Sir Percy Blakeney, who would go on to rescue French aristocrats from the guillotine during the Reign of Terror.

She had been to see someone at the nearby *Daily Express*, and while waiting on the tube station platform, Sir Percy appeared before her. She wrote, 'Now, of all the dull, prosy places in the world, can you beat an Underground railway station? It was foggy, too, and smelly and cold. But I give you my word that as I was sitting there – yes, I saw – Sir Percy Blakeney just as you know him now.'

He wore 'exquisite clothes', while his slender hands held a spy glass. Orczy described his speech as 'lazy' and 'drawling', his laugh 'quaint'. She does not detail everything she saw and heard – it was 'a mental vision' lasting just seconds – but during those moments the life story of the Pimpernel was revealed to her. The rest of the day remained 'a blur in my mind,' she said, 'but my thoughts were clear enough for me to tell my beloved husband about the wonder that had occurred; the birth of the Scarlet Pimpernel.'

Orczy, who spoke no English when she came to London from Hungary aged 15, wrote the novel – originally envisaged as a play – in five weeks, but it was rejected by a dozen publishers. The play was not a great success in 1903, but the novel was published in 1905, when the play came to London, and was an instant bestseller. It led to three film versions and also television versions.

Address Victoria Embankment, WC2R 2PH, www.tlf.org.uk | Getting there Underground to Temple (Circle and District lines) | Hours See website for tube timetable and opening times | Tip Along Victoria Embankment is Cleopatra's Needle, one of a pair – the other is in New York – made for the Pharaoh Thutmose III in 1460 B.C. in Egypt. It was given to commemorate British victories of The Nile and Alexandria, and arrived in England in 1878. A public subscription of £15,000 paid for the passage.

96 Thackeray's House

Where Vanity Fair was penned

Young Street was not the only Kensington home of William Makepeace Thackeray: nearby Palace Green is now the Israeli embassy. However, this handsome, double-bow-fronted building had the greatest personal and professional significance for him. Numbered 13 when he rented it at £65 a year in June 1846, he compared it to a feudal castle and proudly proclaimed, 'I'll have a flagstaff put over the coping of the wall, and I'll hoist up the standard when I'm at home!' His coming lionisation might justify his pride.

His wife Isabella had suffered from severe depression since 1840 and lived in a private asylum from 1845 until her death in 1893 – by which time he had been dead for 30 years. Thackeray was effectively a widower until the end of his life, but in 1846 his two surviving daughters, 11-year-old Anne and six-year-old Minny (Harriet), came to live in then still semi-rural Kensington, after living with their grandparents in Paris. There were also three servants and a small black cat.

Thackeray attributed the resumption of family life to his being able to complete *Vanity Fair*, published as a book in 1848. He received £1,200 plus a share of the profits, and until the last years of his life his income was more than £7,000 a year. Here, he also published *The History of Pendennis* and *The History of Henry Esmond*, as well as journalism, largely for *Punch*. *Pendennis* was dictated from his first floor bedroom 'while whiffing his cigar' and contains descriptions of nearby Kensington Square during the Jacobite uprising.

Two years after he moved in, Charlotte Brontë attended a dinner party and said very little other than to reply 'Yes' and 'No' when asked if she liked London. After moving to Palace Green, he and a friend passed No. 13 and Thackeray demanded, 'Down on your knees, you rogue, for there is the house where *Vanity Fair* was penned and I will go down with you for I have a high opinion of it myself.'

Address 16 Young Street, W8 5EH | **Getting there** Underground to Kensington High Street (District and Circle lines) | **Hours** Viewing from outside only | **Tip** To see the room where Queen Victoria was born, visit the nearby 17th-century Kensington Palace, which remains home to some members of the Royal Family.

97 Thomas Cromwell's Palace

One of London's largest private residences

Though more than a century separates them, Thomas Cromwell had always stood in the shadow of his prominent distant relative, Oliver Cromwell, who was his great-great-grand-nephew. That is, until Hilary Mantel's *Wolf Hall* trilogy topped the best-seller lists.

Born in Putney in 1485, growing prosperity allowed Cromwell to buy a lease and then the freehold from Augustinian friars. He then rebuilt as his home two gatehouses adjoining their friary's 5.5 acre site. Cromwell lived here with his wife, Elizabeth, and their three children and also the illegitimate Jane (Mantel's Janneke), born in 1530 (Elizabeth and two daughters died in 1529). But his rise in Henry VIII's court by 1532, when he became chief minister, necessitated a home appropriate to his position. Consequently, he purchased several surrounding properties and created one of the largest private residences in London, with 58 rooms and covering two acres. His neighbours included merchants, the ambassadors of France and the Holy Roman Empire, and the Dutch philosopher, Erasmus.

The palace also housed servants and a niece and nephew, all of whom crowd Mantel's pages. There was also Liz's father and stepmother, Henry and Mercy Wykes, her sister, her husband and their daughter. 'It's not a dynasty, he thinks, but it's a start,' the novelist has Cromwell muse. But as Mantel shows a public and private man, so she shows Austin Friars as family home, administrative offices and a palace where he could entertain important guests. Thomas is no longer in the shadow of Oliver, but the great mansion, in the City of London, is no more. The king seized it at Cromwell's fall and three years after his execution in 1540, aged 55, Henry VIII sold the property to the Draper's Company. Used by them for a while partly as their hall, Cromwell's house was lost in the Great Fire of London in 1666 (see ch. 1), though the upper garden survives, with the modern Draper's Hall on the site.

Address Drapers' Hall, Throgmorton Avenue, EC2N 2DQ, +44 (0)207 588 5001, www.thedrapers.co.uk | Getting there Underground to Bank (Northern and Central lines) | Hours Visiting by appointment | Tip The Mansion House, built in 1753, is the home of the Lord Mayor of London. Its Palladian front and Corinthian columns make it one of London's most recognisable sights. Tours take place every Tuesday afternoon; pre-booking required (www.cityoflondon.gov.uk).

98 Tower Hamlets Town Hall

Mark Twain entertains patients

It was a 'glorious' spring day in 1897 when Mark Twain made a surprise visit to what was then the Royal London Hospital – now Tower Hamlets Town Hall. Nine months earlier, following a year-long, round-the-world lecture tour, he had arrived in London. Almost immediately news reached him that his favourite daughter, 24-year-old Susy, was seriously ill in Connecticut. Twain's wife, Livy, and their second-eldest daughter, Clara, returned home, while Twain remained in England; but on 18 August, 1896, Susy died. Alone, exhausted and depressed, Twain turned down requests to lecture, and saw only a few friends. One of these was American Adele Chapin, who, with her husband Robert, Twain had first met at a dinner party in New York. When Robert was American consul in South Africa, they had entertained Twain in Johannesburg. In January 1897, when the Chapins moved to London, their friendship with the novelist was renewed.

Adele remembered how unhappy and restless Twain was at the time. He would pace up and down her living room and say, 'If I was God, I would be ashamed to treat my children so. Don't talk to me about a Heavenly Father; no human father would behave as God does.' Appreciative of her concern for his distress, she recalled him saying, 'Do you know, I believe I would do almost anything you wanted me to do.' She worked as a volunteer at the hospital and was herself grateful to the hospital for its care of her seriously ill children shortly before. Now she held Twain to his promise, and asked if he would entertain the patients.

In his inimitable way, he told tall tales of his own childhood, along with a variety of amusing anecdotes, with two 'charming young ladies' from the hospital's Music Society accompanying him on piano and violin. It gave solace to Twain as it brightened the lives of seriously ill and dying patients. It was his greatest performance.

Address Whitechapel Road, E1 1BJ, +44 (0)207 364 5000, www.townhamlets.gov.uk | Getting there Overground and Underground to Whitechapel (Elizabeth and Hammersmith & City lines) or Underground to Stepney Green (Hammersmith & City and District lines) | Hours Viewable 24 hours | Tip In Mile End Road stands a statue of one of the greatest of religious reformers: William Booth, founder of the Salvation Army.

99 Tower Hill

Where the author of Utopia met his death

Sir Thomas More displayed his characteristic humour when mounting the scaffold at Tower Hill on 6 July, 1635. He told the governor of the Tower of London, 'I pray you, see me safe up, and for my coming down let me shift for myself.' Today, a plaque and small garden on Tower Hill, near the Tower, commemorate his end, and that of others executed there.

More was taken to the Tower when writing his *Treatise on the Passion* – one of several books he wrote, the most famous of which is *Utopia*. A satirical work of fiction, published in 1615, it depicts life on an island, and details, in the words of its full title, 'a republic's best state'. More coined the word for the title and the book remains influential today, the word in common use.

More, who was made a saint in 1935, rose to become Henry VIII's Lord Chancellor, but when his Catholic faith did not allow him to acknowledge the king as head of the Church of England, or the annulment of his marriage to Catherine of Aragon, More was tried for treason. The cell from which he was taken to his death is disputed, and he may have spent time in several cells. His biographer, Peter Ackroyd, says that More's cell had a vaulted ceiling, a flagstone floor, a table, chair, pallet bed, and a small brick stove.

More was allowed to walk in the Tower's garden and its 'liberties' – the small neighbourhood that surrounded the castle. He wore a hair-shirt, had a psalter and other devotional books; he prayed and, on appropriate days, sang hymns. He wrote his *Dialogue of Comfort Against Tribulation*, letters and rhymes, some not without humour. To his daughter, Margaret, who visited him, as later did his wife, Dame Anne, More wrote soon after entering: 'I am in good health and body, and quiet of mind.' His body was buried in an unmarked grave, but his head lies in a chapel in the Anglican church of St Dunstan, Canterbury.

Sir William Stanley, K.G. 1495
James Tuchet, 7th Baron Audley 1497
Edward Plantagenet, Earl of Warwick 1499
Edward Stafford, 3rd Duke of Buckingham 1521
John Fisher, Bishop of Rochester 1535
Sir Thomas More 1535
Thomas Darcy, Lord Darcy of Templehurst, K.G. 1537

Address EC3N 4SG, +44 (0)333 320 6000, www.hrp.org.uk | Getting there Underground to Tower Hill (District and Circle lines) | Hours Unrestricted | Tip The Yeomen of the Guard ('Beefeaters') are members of the monarch's bodyguard and ceremonial guardians of the Tower. Join them on a conducted tour of the tower, built in 1086 (www.hrp.org.uk).

100 The Trafalgar Tavern

George Eliot celebrates

In 1861, George Eliot was given a rare, even unique, honour – she was invited to a celebratory whitebait fish dinner to mark the completion of her third novel, *Silas Marner*. Eliot had found some success with her short stories, *Scenes from Clerical Life*, but became a best-selling author with the novels *Adam Bede* and *Mill on the Floss*. *Silas Marner* was her shortest novel, and one with a happy ending, featuring a miser who turns philanthropist and adopts a child. Eight thousand copies were sold by the end of 1861, and its author was £1,760 better off. Her real name was Mary Ann Evans, but she wrote as George Eliot because Marian Evans was known as a radical and free-thinking novelist who lived with the critic George Henry Lewes, a married man.

Eliot was the only woman present at the dinner, and it is not known that any other women received such an accolade. However, Eliot's position as a 'fallen woman' seems not to have prejudiced the guests, for while Victorian society allowed men to be in the company of such a woman, other women could not.

The tradition of a whitebait dinner at the Trafalgar Tavern to mark an author's completion of a novel was instigated in 1851 by the now forgotten but then popular historical novelist William Harrison Ainsworth. He invited friends to the first such event when he finished *Mervyn Clitheroe*. Others who became regular attendees included Charles Dickens (see ch. 19), Wilkie Collins and William Makepeace Thackeray (see ch. 96). Charlie, the 24-year-old son of Dickens, and himself a future writer and journalist, attended once and ended up the worse for drink. Henry James enjoyed himself, if in a more sedate way than young Charlie: 'I would try to express how pleasant it may be to sit in the company of clever and distinguished men before the large windows that look upon the broad brown Thames' – a view that today's visitors may still enjoy.

Address Park Row, SE10 9NW, +44 (0)207 887 9886, www.trafalgartavern.co.uk | Getting there Train to Maze Hill or DLR to Cutty Sark | Hours See website for opening hours | Tip Leave the tavern by boat from Greenwich Pier, and explore London on the river, from Barking in the east to Putney in the west.

101 University College

Jeremy Bentham in his own image

Some may hope that a plaque, tablet, statue or other type of memorial will attest to their fame for future generations. Not so the writer and philosopher Jeremy Bentham. Three months before he died in 1832, at the age of 85, he instructed that 'a man in his own image', or what he called an 'auto-icon', be created using parts of his body. Not that he was lacking other lasting memorials: he left 30 million words unpublished at his death. One of the most well-known philosophers and social reformers, he proposed prison reform with his 'panopticon', a prison with a central hall and radial wings, which influenced prison design in the UK, USA, Netherlands and Cuba. Other of his ideas were his advocacy of free universal education, universal suffrage, and the legalisation of homosexuality. Most famously, he formulated the philosophy of utilitarianism, which propounds the idea of 'the greatest happiness of the greatest number … the measure of right and wrong'.

There could be no more appropriate place for the auto-icon than University College London, for his ideas influenced those who founded the university (as London University) in 1826, and he bought share number 633 for £100. UCL was founded as a secular establishment – an alternative to Anglican Oxford and Cambridge – and was the first to admit students regardless of their religion, as well as the first to admit women.

Bentham has been in the university since 1850, thoughtfully seated in his favourite chair, wearing his usual clothes. However, there is no corpse: beneath the clothes is straw, as he donated his organs to medical research. He did leave his head for the icon, but, although mummified, after 10 years it had deteriorated, and had to be replaced by today's more acceptable alternative. For many years, the head sat between his legs, but since 1975 it has been stored in the university's vaults.

Address Gower Street, WC1E 6BT, +44 (0)207 679 2000 www.ucl.ac.uk | Getting there Underground to Goodge Street (Northern and Elizabeth lines) or Euston Square (Circle, Hammersmith & City, and Metropolitan lines) | Hours Daily 7am–7pm | Tip Off parallel Woburn Place is Woburn Walk, a short, attractive thoroughfare, designed by Thomas Cubitt as one of the first pedestrianised streets. It has the unusual distinction that the writers W. B. Yeats and Dorothy Richardson lived opposite one another around the turn of the 20th century.

102 Victoria & Albert Museum

H. G. Wells finds his way

Although H. G. Wells was a well-read and an imaginative writer from a young age, he seemed destined for a draper's life and a teaching career. But in 1885, when working as an assistant teacher in Sussex, he won a year-long government studentship to the South Kensington Normal School of Science – a teacher training college to degree level – with the chance of a two-year scholarship, which he achieved.

In what became the Royal College of Science – now part of Imperial College – he was taught the sciences by T. H. Huxley, defender of Darwin (see ch. 28). Wells was 18, short and under nourished, weighing only seven stone, and shabbily dressed. It was his first time living in London, mostly with his Aunt Mary and cousin, Isabel ('Jane'), whom he would later marry. According to one biographer, Wells took to his studies 'like a parched traveller at last reaching water', in what was both a new intellectual and social world: he gained new knowledge, learned about method and observation, joined the debating society, attended the Fabian Society, which made him a socialist, and set up a student journal. However, when he could no longer study zoology he realised that literature and history interested him, rather than geology and physics.

After failing to get a degree in 1887, Wells went to teach at an impoverished boarding school in Wales. He later returned to London, obtained a degree, married, and started writing journalism. A decade later, he found fame with *The Time Machine*. Within six years, he had published five other science fiction books, including *The Invisible Man* and *The War of the Worlds*, as well as other books. Wells eventually became one of the great popularisers of history and science. His time at the Normal School may have ended in academic failure, but, in many ways, it was the making of one of the 20th century's greatest writers.

Address Henry Cole Wing (now part of the V&A) was the Normal School, Exhibition Road, SW7 2PA, +44 (0)20 7942 2000, www.vam.ac.uk | Getting there Underground to South Kensington (Piccadilly, District, and Circle lines) | Hours Mon–Thu 10am–5.45pm, Fri 10am–8pm | Tip North of the V&A is the Royal Geographical Society in Lowther Lodge, designed by Norman Shaw. This learned society was founded in 1830, and is open to non-members for occasional exhibitions and lectures (www.rgs.org).

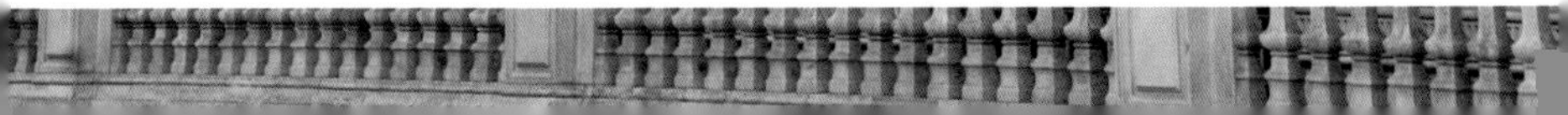

103 Victoria Park Square

Deedes of war

In 1936, 23-year-old Bill Deedes, later author, newspaper editor, MP, government minister, and member of the House of Lords, set out from 18 Victoria Park Square, using two taxis. He took 600 pounds of luggage for a two-week journey to Abyssinia, as correspondent for the *Morning Post* covering the war provoked by the Italian invasion. From 1931 to 1939, he shared the handsome house with his uncle, Brigadier-General Sir Wyndham Deedes, a former senior colonial civil servant, who had secured the young Deedes a post on the newspaper, despite his nephew lacking journalistic experience.

Before Deedes departed, as the amount of luggage suggests, he went on a 'shopping spree' – and at the end of his life, in 2007, one of his well-made, silk-lined tropical suits, with safari jacket with four pockets, hung in his wardrobe. However, while this journey was the making of him as a journalist, it also gave him an unusual and enduring fame, though he said he spent part of his life 'brushing away the charge'.

The novelist Evelyn Waugh (see ch. 30) arrived at the same time, also as a correspondent. In *Scoop*, he based William Boot, the hapless gardening correspondent of the *Daily Beast* who is mistaken for a war correspondent, on Deedes. Waugh had great fun with Deedes' extensive wardrobe and sporting equipment (hockey and polo sticks!). Deedes admitted: 'My inexperience and naïvety as a reporter in Africa might have contributed a few bricks to the building of Boot.' Naïve and inexperienced as he may have been, after his death, the Ethiopian ambassador stated that Deedes' sharp journalistic instincts ensured Italian excesses were kept in the public eye.

Deedes, later editor of the *Daily Telegraph*, retained a lifelong concern for Africa, and was there in his 80s, campaigning against landmines. His last article appeared 14 days before his death – it was about the genocidal cruel war in Darfur.

Address 18 Victoria Park Square, E2 9PF | **Getting there** Underground to Bethnal Green (Central line) | **Hours** Viewable from outside only | **Tip** Nearby Victoria Park, the oldest public park in Britain, was opened in 1845 as the 'People's Park'. It is a green corridor in a highly populated area, with a range of community activities, events, live music and sports.

104 Vigo Street

Literary building where a Penguin flew in

8 Vigo Street has a long association with publishing, but is best known as the first home of arguably the most influential publishing house ever created: in 1935 Sir Allen Lane, with cousins John and Richard, founded Penguin. The imprint was at first an off-shoot of The Bodley Head, which Lane's uncle, John Lane, had created in 1887 in Vigo Street. Lane joined in 1919 and changed his name, in deference to his uncle, from Williams, as did his parents, brother and sister.

Lane became a director in 1925, on his uncle's death, and chairman in 1930, but often clashed with the board of what had become a rather staid company. He eventually secured Bodley Head's publication of James Joyce's *Ulysses* (see ch. 14) in 1936, after other directors feared a prosecution that never happened. But Lane now saw that if he was to be an innovative publisher, it was unlikely to be at The Bodley Head.

He got the idea for Penguin when he could not find anything to read at Exeter railway station, and saw the need for cheap, good quality, well-designed contemporary books.

Penguin was not the first publisher of paperbacks, but its books were the first to be aimed at the mass market, at an inexpensive 6d (2 1/2p). They were certainly the first such books of quality, in terms of both content and production. Agatha Christie and Ernest Hemingway were on the first list that soon extended to the classics.

The famed symbol was chosen by Lane as 'dignified but flippant', after being suggested by a secretary, and created by a 21-year-old office junior. The first order was for only 7,000 copies until Woolworth's – a popular store not known for selling literature – came to the rescue with an order of 63,000 copies. This allowed Lane to separate from the Bodley Head in 1936. A plaque on this pleasant, bow-fronted building states without exaggeration that Penguin 'changed the reading habits of the English-speaking world'.

Address 8 Vigo Street, W1S 3HJ | Getting there Underground to Piccadilly Circus (Piccadilly and Bakerloo lines) | Hours Viewable from outside only | Tip Step back to the grandeur of Regent Street. Later reconstruction has taken most of the buildings of John Nash and James Burton but their sweeping design, named for the Prince Regent (later George IV), is now home to leading brand shops, mainly for clothing.

105_Wardour Street

Where feminist publishing began

Feminist publishing company Virago first appeared in 1972, briefly as Spare Rib Books, changing its name in 1973. Its first book, *Fenwomen* by Mary Chamberlain, came out in 1975. In between times its office was the Chelsea flat of one of its founders, Carmen Calill, from which the first 10 books were published, in association with Quartet Books. It became an independent company backed by gifts, loans and £1,500 capital. Two years later, Virago moved to the fourth floor of No. 5. It was an inauspicious move: 'a one room walk-up at a dubious address in Soho', as the author Margaret Atwood remembered it.

Scruffy, linoleum-covered stairs, closed doors, a hairdresser, and a men's drinking club led to the office. This was a large room, with two tables, three telephones, three electric typewriters, filing cabinets, a small kitchen and a toilet down a corridor. Three staff were joined by two more within a year.

In 1978, Virago published its first Virago Classic: *Frost in May* by Antonia White (see ch. 42). While the house brought back into print neglected books by women, it was also publishing original titles from the start. The company published both new and established women writers, but it also published works with feminist themes written by male authors, such as H. G. Wells (see ch. 102).

Virago went to a new home in 1981, sharing office space in Mayfair with Oxford University Press. The next year it became a wholly owned subsidiary of Chatto & Windus, and later part of the Random House group. In 2006, the imprint was taken over by Hachette Livre. Since its inception there have been new authors launched, classic books rediscovered, and ventures such as the travel series. After over half a century, and over 4,000 titles by more than 1,000 authors, its founding principle remains: to bring feminist literature into the mainstream, for male and female readers alike.

Address 5 Wardour Street, W1D 6DP | **Getting there** Underground to Piccadilly Circus (Piccadilly and Bakerloo lines) | **Hours** Viewable from outside only | **Tip** In the south-east corner of Trafalgar Square is Admiralty Arch, a stunning structure, commissioned by Edward VII to commemorate his mother Queen Victoria, and soon to be a hotel.

106 W. B. Yeats Sculpture

Nobel Prize winner's early years in London

In 1867, when he was two years old, Dublin-born W. B. Yeats moved to London with his parents and three siblings. There are two official blue plaques that commemorate his years in the capital, at the poet's homes in Bloomsbury and Primrose Hill. At 3 Blenheim Road, Chiswick, where he spent his formative years, there's also a plaque placed by the local civic society. But it took several years for the Irish national poet and Nobel Prize winner to have more visible recognition in the form of a sculpture.

The family came to London after Yeats' father, Jack, switched from being a barrister to being a painter. At first the children were educated at home, but in 1877 Yeats was enrolled at the Godolphin School, Hammersmith. Having lived in Fulham, the family came to Bedford Park in 1879. It was conveniently near then semi-rural parts, and within easy reach of the capital for Jack, for galleries and clients, by way of the new District line station at Turnham Green. They then moved back to Ireland, but returned to Bedford Park in 1888, this time to Blenheim Road.

It was here that Yeats wrote one of his most famous poems, *The Lake Isle of Innisfree*, and met Maud Gonne when she came to visit, and with whom Yeats fell in love. The couple never married, but Gonne inspired much of his work. The family had the house until 1902, when they once again returned to Ireland.

After much campaigning, in September 2022 a sculpture was unveiled at the entrance to Bedford Park. At the base of the abstract work are words from one of Yeats' most famous poems, *He Wishes for the Cloths of Heaven*. However, it is not the poem's famous final line that is quoted – 'tread softly because you tread on my dreams' – but instead the lines 'Had I but heavens' embroidered cloths / Enwrought with golden and silver light / The blue and the dim and the dark cloths / Of night and light and the half light…'.

Address Bath Road, W4 1TT | Getting there Underground to Turnham Green (Piccadilly and District lines) | Hours Viewable 24 hours | Tip Treat yourself to a liquid break and learn all about gin at the Sipsmith Gin Distillery (https://sipsmith.com).

107 Westminster Bridge

From here, Wordsworth's 'sight so touching'

William Wordsworth is associated with the Lake District, and much of his poetry, like *Tintern Abbey* and *Daffodils*, reflects the countryside and rural life. But *Composed upon Westminster Bridge*, one of his most famous poems, is a tribute to the London townscape, 'a hymn to a still and silent London', in the words of biographer Juliet Barker. Maybe now, with skyscrapers in both directions along much of the banks of the Thames and in the City itself, the modern reader may think that Earth has few less things to show more fair; and one would not be dull of soul 'who could pass by / A sight so touching in its majesty'. However, to cross Westminster Bridge is to be at the centre of one of the world's great cities, and with some imagination it is not difficult to see why the poet wrote as he did.

Wordsworth's sister, Dorothy, tells how she and her brother left London very early on the morning of 3 September, 1802 on the Dover coach from Charing Cross – six decades before the creation of the railway station – for the boat to Calais, and 'made a most beautiful sight as we crossed Westminster Bridge'. Her diary noted, 'The houses were not overhung by their cloud of smoke & they were spread out endlessly, yet the sun shone so brightly with such a pure light that there was even something like the purity of one of nature's own grand Spectacles.' Today, smoke is what the London traveller rarely, if ever, sees.

Wordsworth seems to have written the poem that day or the next, and its enduring appeal is partly that it sums up moments in the eye of a great poet, who wrote it with simplicity and beauty.

'The river glideth at his own sweet will / Dear God! the very houses seem asleep' still seems, despite the present-day townscape, to catch London at a very early hour, the expanse of the city – much smaller then than now – and the winding Thames, running off to the sea.

Address Westminster Bridge, SE1 | Getting there Underground to Westminster (Jubilee, District and Circle lines) | Hours Unrestricted | Tip Parliament Square (SW1P 3JX) is more than a large, grassy roundabout in front of the Houses of Parliament. To be found there are statues of Nelson Mandela, General Smuts, Gandhi, David Lloyd George, Millicent Garrett Anderson, and Abraham Lincoln – a replica of the one in Chicago's Lincoln Park.

108_The Wheatsheaf

The artist, his model and the poet

In the spring of 1936, 58-year-old painter Augustus John introduced his 22-year-old lover Caitlin McNamara, who was also a model and a dancer, to Dylan Thomas in this well-known Fitzrovian pub. Thomas was making a trip to London and Caitlin had just returned from Paris. She had an unrequited love for one of John's sons, an emotion she then switched to the father. Although she denied years later that she ever loved John, their relationship was undoubtedly sexual, and, for a while after meeting Thomas, she continued to sleep with John. She never claimed that John was ever faithful to her – he slept, she said, with all his models, whatever their age and status. Thomas was the opposite. 'Caitlin, Caitlin, I love you. I can't tell you how much,' runs one letter shortly before their marriage.

'Come and meet someone rather amusing,' John said to Caitlin. She, 'quite mute', nervously approached the 21-year-old Welsh poet. Ever-impecunious, Thomas still immediately proposed to her, and ten minutes later they were in bed above the Eiffel Tower restaurant and hotel in nearby Percy Street, spending the night there and putting everything on John's account. There was no 'handing over' of Caitlin from John to Thomas. The men undoubtedly showed jealousy so far as she was concerned, and she feared that John might find out, so the poet and dancer parted – he to Cornwall and she to Hampshire.

Whatever the tripartite complications of the relationship, Caitlin and Thomas married in July 1937 in the new register office in Penzance in Cornwall. It was the beginning of a tempestuous marriage – 'raw, red, bleeding meat', as Thomas characterised it. The marriage ended only with Thomas' death while in a coma in New York in 1953, resulting from swollen brain tissue and pneumonia, exacerbated by heavy drinking. She lived another 41 years, the last 20 of them without touching alcohol.

Address 25 Rathbone Place, W1T 1JB, +44 (0)207 580 1585, www.thewheatsheaffitzrovia.co.uk | **Getting there** Underground to Tottenham Court Road (Elizabeth, Central and Northern lines) | **Hours** Mon–Sat noon–11pm, Sun 4–10pm | **Tip** On the other side of Oxford Street is the Photographers' Gallery, founded in 1971 as the first public gallery devoted solely to photography. It has various exhibitions, a café, gift shop and bookshop.

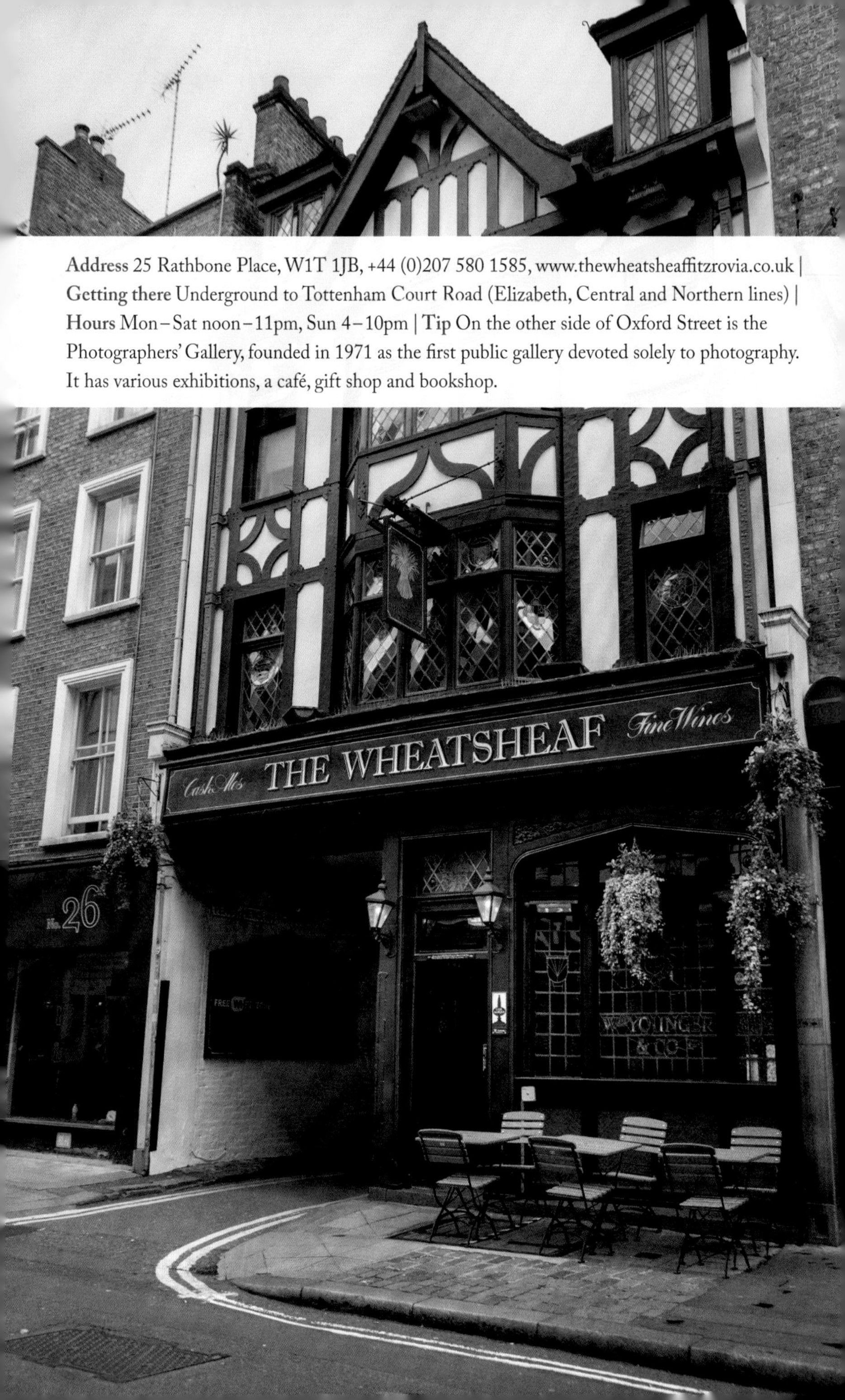

109 Wiener Holocaust Library

Mystery about the world's most infamous book

The origins of the oldest Holocaust library in the world lie in 1920s Germany. A concerned Dr Alfred Wiener started collecting posters, newsletters, books and assorted memorabilia about growing antisemitism, the rise of right-wing groups and militia and, eventually, the Nazis. His collection is the great-grandparent of today's holdings, which include 80,000 books, magazines, and pamphlets, 45,000 photographs, 2,000 documents, 3,000 periodicals, one million press cuttings, as well as oral histories, scrapbooks, pamphlets, film and posters. There are books in French, Hebrew, English, Yiddish, German, Russian and other languages, that cannot be found elsewhere. The library has several copies of *Mein Kampf.* These are mostly in German, but one in English is signed by the author, Adolf Hitler, and has a curious history.

It is not known how the library obtained the book, but there is a clue to its origins. There is a photograph inside showing a group of people gathered around Hitler and other Nazis, including someone who appears to be his secretary, Martin Bormann. In the group a young, blonde woman in a white dress is smiling. Beneath the photograph are lines written in pencil by (it is assumed) the young woman. She tells of visiting Berchtesgaden, near Hitler's mountain-top summer home, and relates how he came to the village to shake hands with tourists. She adds, 'Signed in pencil standing up! Just before we were evacuated.'

Thus, it seems the young woman was a tourist who took an English translation of the book to Germany, apparently in the hope that she would see Hitler and he would sign it. Perhaps she was naïve in her youth, or maybe she was a Nazi sympathiser. Interesting as the signature is, the story of its owner – and why she was visiting Hitler's now infamous retreat on the eve of war – will always be an intriguing mystery.

Address 29 Russell Square, WC1B 5DP, +44 (0)20 7636 7247, www.wienerholocaustlibrary.org | Getting there Underground to Russell Square (Piccadilly line) | Hours Mon–Fri 10–5pm; free tours Tue 2pm | Tip Grab a bite and a drink at the cabbies' green-painted, wooden shelter directly opposite the library; look out for these little-noticed but iconic places dotted around the capital.

110 William Morris Gallery

Bringing beauty back to printing

William Morris, writer, designer of fabrics and wallpapers, and pioneer socialist, was born here in 1838 in what was then a village. While the family moved to a grand house on the edge of Epping Forest when he was six, the area cast a spell over later life. In Morris's *News from Nowhere* (1890), the 21st century Dick shows the time-traveller and narrator William Guest around the area after Guest's 160-year-long sleep and a mid 20th-century socialist revolution. He calls it, 'A pretty place, too; a very jolly place, now that the trees have had time to grow again since the great clearing of houses in 1952.'

The gallery is full of books, items of furniture and memorabilia, but one of the most important items is a first edition of the *Kelmscott Chaucer*, published by Morris in 1896 on his own Kelmscott Press, founded in 1891. With 87 wood-cut illustrations by Edward Burne-Jones, the book is an example of Morris' attempt to bring beauty to the printing of books. It exemplifies his wish that the press should revive the skills of hand printing, which mechanisation had destroyed, and restore the quality of 15th-century printing. The illustrations were engraved and printed in black, with shoulder and side titles. Some lines are in red, using Chaucer type, some titles in Morris' Troy type, and the text type is from Venice of the 1470s. The whole was printed on Perch, a handmade, watermarked paper, using specially acquired ink from Germany.

Morris died in 1896, and the book was the last great achievement of his life. It combined his love of medieval literature and his socialist philosophy, which looked back to a time before the division of labour and mechanisation. Morris believed that these had destroyed personal fulfilment and the social function of meaningful work. There are few better illustrations of Morris' social, political and creative outlook.

Address Lloyd Park, Forest Road, E17 4PP, +44 (0)207 496 4390, www.wmgallery.org.uk | Getting there Train or Underground to Walthamstow Central (Victoria line) | Hours Tue–Sun 10am–5pm; entry is free | Tip Walthamstow Pumphouse Museum is a Grade II-listed Victorian pumping station, opened by enthusiasts in 1997. There are displays of firefighting equipment, tube carriages and a modern railway (www.walthamstowpumphouse.org.uk).

111 Winston Churchill's Home

Statesman's years at Hyde Park Gate

Sir Winston Churchill bought 28 Hyde Park Gate in 1945 when he was rejected from office after his war-time term as prime minister. By then an MP for 45 years, this was Churchill's 21st London home, and would be the London home where he lived longest. Before becoming premier, he served in various cabinet posts, including as Home Secretary and Chancellor of the Exchequer, under Herbert Asquith (he resigned after the Battle of Gallipoli in 1915), David Lloyd George, Stanley Baldwin, and Neville Chamberlain.

Hyde Park Gate was the home where he served his only term as leader of the Opposition (1945-1951) and his last term as prime minister (1951-1955). A visitor described waiting in 'a beautiful room with bookshelves let into the wall and carrying superb bound volumes of French and English books.' There were pictures of Churchill's ancestor, the Duke of Marlborough, and John Lavery's First World War portrait of Churchill. Since his days as a young officer and war correspondent he had been a prolific author. In 1953, while prime minister, he was awarded the Nobel Prize for Literature.

After his resignation in 1955, Churchill retained Hyde Park Gate, but bought No. 27 next door as an office. He had always spent much of his time at his beloved Chartwell in Kent, but post-war years were ones of frequent travel, often on painting holidays. He also revised his book *History of the English-Speaking Peoples*. On 30 November, 1964, Churchill's 90th birthday, crowds gathered outside the house to sing 'Happy birthday', and he appeared at an upstairs window to give his famous Victory sign. Having suffered several strokes, he died at Hyde Park Gate on 24 January 1965. He was accorded the rare honour, for a commoner, of a state funeral.

Address 28 Hyde Park Gate, SW7 5DJ | Getting there Underground to Knightsbridge (Piccadilly line) | Hours Always visible from outside only | Tip On the north-east corner of Hyde Park you'll find the Horse at Water, an impressive 10 metre bronze sculpture weighing over 100kg.

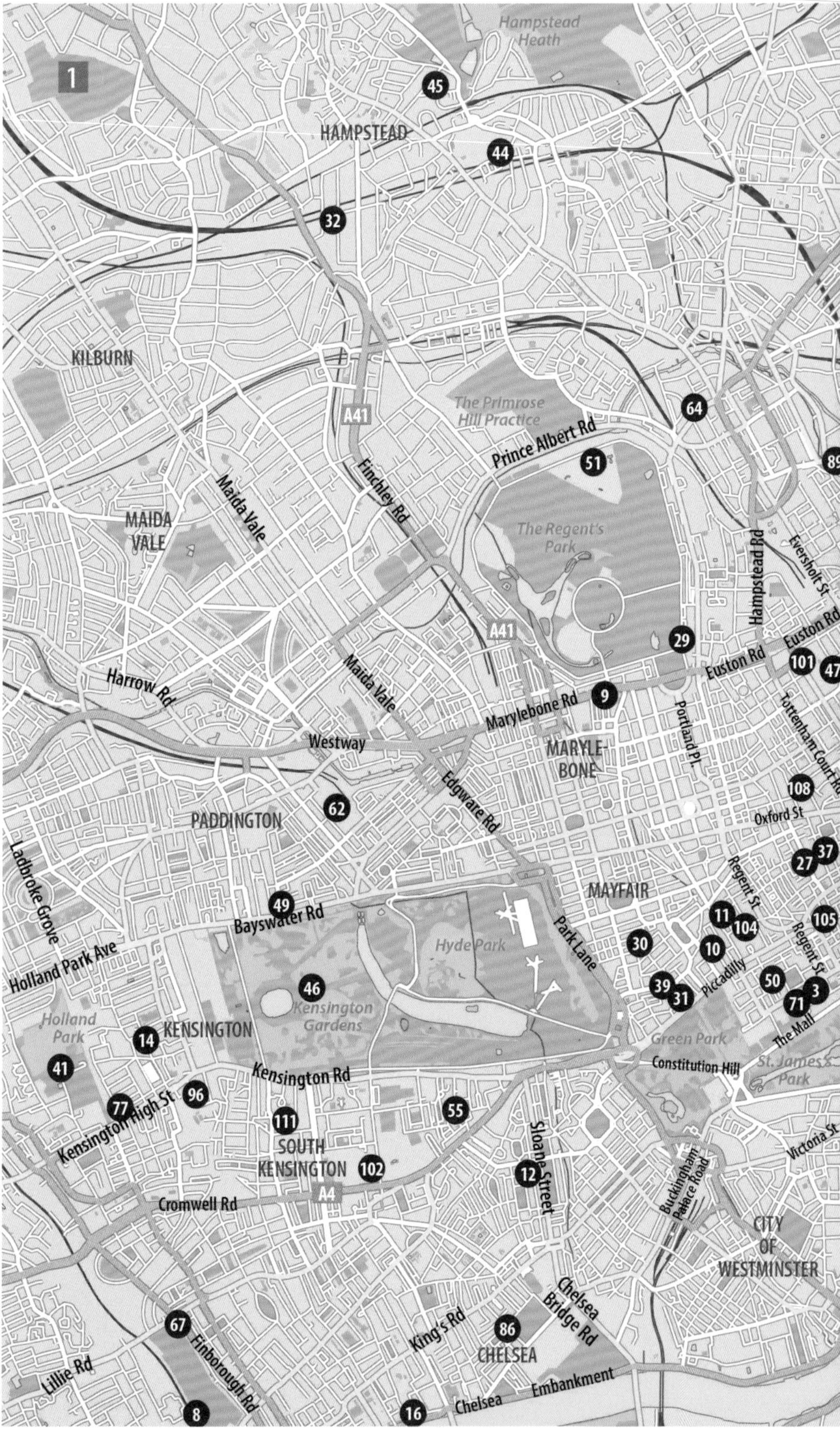

1
Hampstead Heath
45
HAMPSTEAD
44
32
KILBURN
A41
The Primrose Hill Practice
64
Prince Albert Rd
51
89
Finchley Rd
Maida Vale
MAIDA VALE
The Regent's Park
Hampstead Rd
Eversholt St
A41
29
Euston Rd
Euston Rd
101
47
Harrow Rd
Maida Vale
Marylebone Rd
9
Portland Pl.
Tottenham Court Rd
Westway
MARYLE-BONE
Edgware Rd
108
62
PADDINGTON
Oxford St
Ladbroke Grove
37
27
Regent St
MAYFAIR
49
Bayswater Rd
11
104
105
Park Lane
Hyde Park
30
10
Regent St
Holland Park Ave
Piccadilly
46
39
31
50
3
Kensington Gardens
71
Holland Park
The Mall
14
KENSINGTON
Green Park
41
Constitution Hill
St. James's Park
Kensington Rd
96
77
Kensington High St
55
111
Sloane Street
Victoria St
SOUTH KENSINGTON
102
12
Buckingham Palace Road
A4
Cromwell Rd
CITY OF WESTMINSTER
Chelsea Bridge Rd
67
86
King's Rd
Finborough Rd
CHELSEA
Lillie Rd
Chelsea Embankment
8
16

2
HOLLOWAY
STOKE NEWINGTON
HACKNEY
A1
A10
Upper St
New North Rd
Kingsland Rd
Pancras Rd
Pentonville Rd
Hackney Rd
City Rd
BETHNAL GREEN
Gray's Inn Rd
Goswell Rd
Old St
Shoreditch
Bethnal Green Rd
Cambridge Heath Rd
Russell Square
Theobalds Rd
Aldersgate Rd
City Rd
Bishopsgate
High Holborn
New Oxford St
Kingsway
London Wall
Whitechapel Rd
A11
A13
Newgate St
Mansell St
Victoria Embankment
Blackfriars Bridge
Southwark Bridge
Upper Thames St
London Bridge
Waterloo Bridge
The Highway
Tower Bridge
Trafalgar Square
Victoria Embankment
Whitehall
Southwark
Tooley St
St Thomas St
York Rd
Borough High
Waterloo Rd
Blackfriars Rd
Westminster Bridge
Borough Rd
Jamaica Rd
SOUTHWARK
Abingdon St
Lambeth Rd
KENNING-TON
WALWORTH
58
15
26
7
2
43
103
59
19
53
76
109
85
78
33
22
20
98
34
80
82
36
61
97
83
90
4
24
81
13
94
54
25
93
60
73
95
17
38
1
99
57
18
79
56
74
107
68
92
48
42

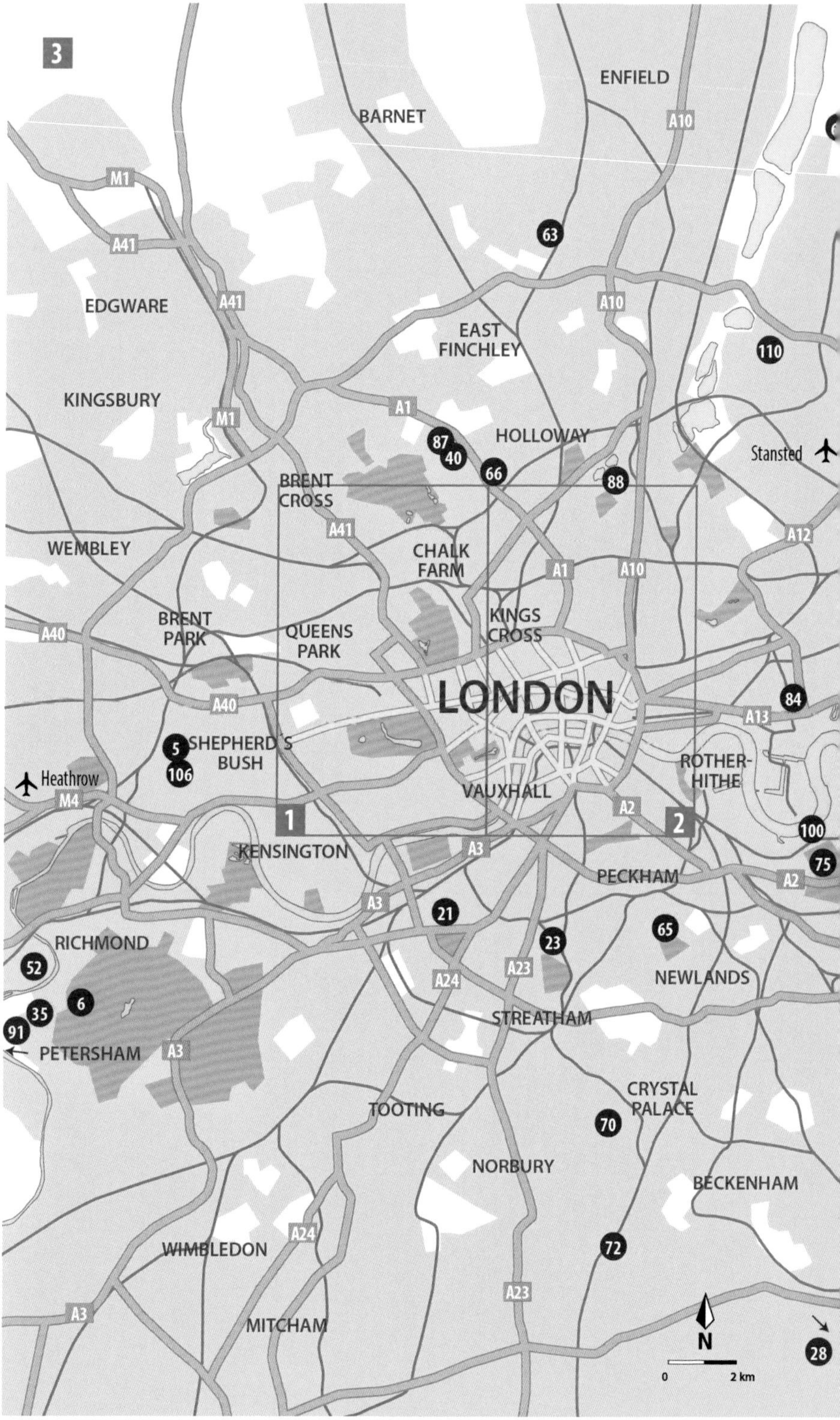
3
ENFIELD
BARNET
A10
M1
63
A41
EDGWARE
A41
A10
EAST
FINCHLEY
110
KINGSBURY
A1
M1
HOLLOWAY
87
40
66
88
Stansted
BRENT
CROSS
A41
A12
WEMBLEY
CHALK
FARM
A1
A10
BRENT
PARK
QUEENS
PARK
KINGS
CROSS
A40
LONDON
84
A40
A13
5
SHEPHERD'S
BUSH
106
Heathrow
M4
ROTHER-
HITHE
VAUXHALL
A2
1
2
100
KENSINGTON
A3
75
PECKHAM
A2
A3
21
65
RICHMOND
23
52
A24
A23
NEWLANDS
6
35
STREATHAM
91
PETERSHAM
A3
CRYSTAL
PALACE
TOOTING
70
NORBURY
BECKENHAM
A24
WIMBLEDON
72
A23
A3
N
MITCHAM
28
0
2 km

Bibliography

My first thanks are due to the always helpful staff of the British Library, to the Surrey library services, and the archives centre of Westminster City Council. Once again, the *Oxford Dictionary of National Biography* was invaluable. In addition to books mentioned in the text, I have read or consulted the following:

Ackroyd, Peter, *Dickens* (London: Sinclair-Stevenson, 1990); Ackroyd, Peter, *Blake* (London: Minerva,1996); Ackroyd, Peter, *Shakespeare* (London: Chatto & Windus, 2005); Aldiss, Brian, Introduction to Verne, Jules, *Around the World in Eighty Days* (London: Penguin Books, 2004); Baines, Jocelyn, *Joseph Conrad: A Critical Biography* (London: Penguin Books, 1960); Barker, Juliet, *William Wordsworth: A Life* (London: Viking, 2000); Barlthrop, Robert, *Jack London: The Man, the Writer, the Rebel* (London: Pluto Press, 1976); Burke, David, *Lawn Road Flats: Spies, Writers and Artists* (Woodbridge: Boydell & Brewer, 2014); Cole, Emily, *Lived in London: Blue Plaques and the Stories Behind Them* (London and New Haven: Yale University Press, 2009);Crawford, Robert, *Eliot: After the Waste Land* (London: Jonathan Cape, 2022); Cunningham, Ian, *A Reader's Guide to Writers' London*. (London: Prion Books, 2001); Deedes, William, *At War with Waugh* (London: Macmillan, 2003); Donovan, Patrick, *Arnold Bennett: Lost Icon* (Lewes: Unicorn Publishing, 2022); Dunn, Jane, *Antonia White: A Life*. (London: Jonathan Cape, 1998); Eagle, Dorothy & Carnell, Hilary, *The Oxford Illustrated Literary Guide to Great Britain and Ireland* (second edition edited by Eagle, Dorothy & Stephens, Meric) (Oxford: OUP, 1992); French, Peter J., *John Dee: The World of an Elizabethan Magus* (London: Routledge & Kegan Paul, 1972); Glendinning, Victoria, *Trollope* (London: Pimlico, 1993); Glinert, Ed, *A Literary Guide to London* (London: Penguin Books, 2000); Glinert, Ed, *The London Compendium* (London: Penguin Books, 2004); Goodings, Lennie, *A Bite of the Apple: A Life with Books, Writers and Virago* (Oxford: Oxford University Press, 2020); Griffith-Jones, Robin, *The Da Vinci Code and the Secrets of the Temple*

(Norwich: Canterbury Press, 2006); Hastings, Selina, *The Secret Lives of Somerset Maugham* (London: John Murray, 2010); Hawksley, Lucinda, *Lizzie Siddal* (London: Andre Deutsch, 2004); Hillier, Bevis, *John Betjeman: The Bonus of Laughter* (London: John Murray, 2004); Holroyd, Michael, *Augustus John. Volume 2: The Years of Experience* (London: William Heinemann, 1975); Kahr, Brett, "At 38,000 feet with Dalí's sketch of Freud: My seven-and-a-half hours as a transatlantic courier", *Athene* (magazine of the Freud Museum), 2021-22, pps.24-29; Lane, Margaret, *The Tale of Beatrix Potter* (London: Penguin Books, 1986); Latham, Robert and Matthews, William, *The Diary of Samuel Pepys. Volume VII: 1666* (London, G. Bell and Sons, 1972); Le Bourgeois, John Y. and Evans, Jonathan, "Mark Twain's secret mission to the London Hospital", *The New England Quarterly*, Jun., 2008, Vol. 81, No. 2; Lewis, R.W.B., *Edith Wharton: A Biography* (New York: Fromm International, 1985); Long, David, *A History of London in 50 Lives* (London: Oneworld, 2015); Luckhurst, Robin, Introduction, *Dracula* by Bram Stoker (Oxford: Oxford University Press, 2011); Lycett, Andrew, *Rudyard Kipling* (London: Weidenfeld & Nicolson, 2015); Lyons, Martyn, *Books: A Living History* (London: *Thames & Hudson*, 2011); Mack, Maynard, *Alexander Pope. A Life* (London: Yale University Press and W.W. Norton & Company, 1985); Mackay, Lauren, *The Wolf Hall Companion* (London: Batsford, 2020); Meyers, Jeffrey, *D. H. Lawrence: A Biography* (London: Macmillan, 1990); Miller, Lucasta, *The Bronte Myth* (London: Vintage, 2020); Monaghan, David, *Smiley's Circus: A Guide to the Secret World of John le Carre* (Orbis,1996); Moorehead, Caroline, *Bertrand Russell* (London: Sinclair-Stevenson, 1992); Morgan, Janet, *Agatha Christie: A Biography* (London: HarperCollins, rev. edition, 2017); Murray, Douglas, *Bosie: A Biography of Lord Alfred Douglas* (London: Hodder & Stoughton, 2000); Murray, Nicholas, *Bloomsbury and the Poets* (Prestigne: Rack Press Editions, 2004); Murray, Nicholas, *Real Bloomsbury* (Bridgend: Seren Books, 2010); Murray, Paul, *From the Shadow of* Dracula. *A Life of Bram Stoker* (London: Jonathan Cape, 2004); Palmer, Richard and Brown, Michelle P., *Lambeth Palace Library: Treasures from the*

Collection of the Archbishops of Canterbury (London: Scala Publishers, 2010); Philpot, Terry, *Over Here, Over There: The People and Places that Made the Story of London and the United States* (Step Beach Press, 2019); Ransome, Arthur, *The Autobiography of Arthur Ransome* (London: Century Publishing, 1985); Roberts, Andrew, *Churchill* (London: Allen Lane, 2018); Robinson, Stephen, *The Remarkable Life of Bill Deedes.* (London: Little, Brown, 2008); Rosen, Michael, *The Disappearance of Émile Zola: Love, Literature and the Dreyfus Case (London:* Faber, 2017); Russell, Bertrand, *The Autobiography of Bertrand Russell 1872-1914* (London: Allen & Unwin, 1967); Saikia, Robin, *Blue Guide Literary Companion: London.* (London: Somerset Books, 2011); Schmidt, Shannon McKenna & Rendon, Joni, *Novel Destinations: Literary Landmarks from Jane Austen's Bath to Ernest Hemingway's Key West* (Washington DC: National Geographic Society, 2008); Scammell. Michael, *Koestler: The Indispensable Intellectual.* (London: Faber and Faber 2010); Shapiro, James, *1599: A Year in the Life of Shakespeare* (London: Faber & Faber, 2006); Sherry, Norman, *The Life of Graham Greene: Volume Two: 1939-1955* (London: Jonathan Cape, 1994); Spark, Muriel, *Curriculum Vitae* (London: Constable and Company, 1992); Sturgis, Matthew, *Oscar: A Life* (London: Head of Zeus, 2018); Tagholm, Robert, *Walking Literary London* (London: New Holland Publishers, 2004) Tames, Richard, *A Traveller's History of London* (Moreton-in-Marsh: The Windrush Press, 1992); Taylor, D.J., *Thackeray* (London: Chatto & Windus, 1999); Thevoz, Seth Alexander, *Behind Closed Doors: The Secret Life of London Private Members Clubs* (London: Robinson, 2022); Thomas, Caitlin, *Double Drink Story. My Life with Dylan Thomas* (London: Virago Press, 1998); Tomalin, Claire, *Charles Dickens* (London, Viking, 2011); Tomalin, Claire, *The Young H.G. Wells* (London: Viking, 2021); Trollope, Anthony, *An Autobiography* (London: Penguin Books, 1996); Varlow, Sally, *A Reader's Guide to Writer's Britain* (London: Prion Books, 1997); Jules-Verne, Jean, *Jules Verne* (London: MacDonald & Jane's, 1976); Wheen, Francis, *Karl Marx* (London: Fourth Estate, 2000); Worsley, Lucy, *Jane Austen at Home* (London: Hodder & Stoughton, 2018)

Acknowledgments

Niti Acharya, manager, Hackney Museum; Giuseppe Albano, director, Freud Museum; Poppy Andrews, senior communications officer, National Portrait Gallery; Sam Butler, events manager, Royal Borough of Kensington & Chelsea, English Heritage; Molly Bridge, media relations officer, and Amad Uddin, student centre, University College London; Hugh Cahill, senior librarian, and Camille Koutoulakis, digital officer, Lambeth Palace; Matt Clark, head teacher, Robert Fitzroy Academy, Croydon; Drew Clode, secretary, Coleridge Trust; Rev Canon Stephen Evans, parish priest, St Marylebone Parish Church; Elizabeth Douglas, collections officer, Royal College of Physicians; Penelope Fussell, archivist, The Drapers' Company; Greene King Brewery; Fiona Healey-Hutchinson, assistant director of development, Middle Temple Hall; Kate Jarman, archivist, Barts NHS Trust; Abbey Wells, PA and office manager, School of Arts, Birkbeck College; Horace Liberty, editor of *The Betjemanian;* Grace Long, press officer, Westminster Abbey; Elana Kudelka, commercial events manager, Sir John Soane Museum; Emily Mahon, consultant, Luther Pendragon; Chris McCabe, national poetry librarian, National Poetry Library; Emma Milnes, deputy library, Zoological Society of London; Jack O'Carroll, assistant director of sales, Clermont Hotel Group; Christina Pascoe, venue hire sales manager, commercial, English Heritage; Lishani Ramanayake, media officer, British Library; Fr Dominic Robinson, parish priest of the Church of the Immaculate Conception; Ken Page interpretation officer, City of London (Keats House); Toby Simpson, director, Wiener Holocaust Library; Elaine Stabler, marketing executive, media and communications, London Library; Kate Tatlow, business officer, London & South East Region, Historic England; Nicola Gray, marketing manager, William Morris Gallery; Bethan Wood, marketing and communications manager, Strawberry Hill House and Garden; John Worthen, emeritus professor, School of English, Nottingham University.

Martin Sketchley, copy editor, focussed an eagle eye on the manuscript. Thanks to Robert Philpot for much technical advise and help with proof reading. And for Mary, who knows why.

Last but most certainly not least, I have to thank Laura Olk, project manager for the UK and US for Emons, the publisher of this book, for her great support during its writing, and all at Emons who brought it to the page.

Photo Credits

ch 19: Portrait of Charles Dickens, Wiki Commons; ch 28: Image courtesy of English Heritage; ch 29: Image courtesy of Royal College of Physicians; ch 32: Karin Tearle, © Salvador Dalí, Fundació Gala-Salvador Dalí/VG Bild-Kunst, Bonn 2023; ch 35: Portrait of John Henry Newman, John Everett Millais/Wiki Commons; ch 36: David Illife/Wiki Commons; ch 45: Image courtesy of Keats House, City of London Corporation; ch 48: Gutenberg Bible, image courtesy of Lambeth Palace Library; ch 50: Small books, London Library, image courtesy of the London Library; ch 51: Drawings by Edward Lear, image courtesy of the Zoological Society of London; ch 52: Karin Tearle, courtesy of Marble Hill House & Garden managed by English Heritage; ch 53: Karin Tearle, image courtesy Marx Memorial Library, artwork by Jack Hastings; ch 57: Portrait of Jane Austen, image courtesy © National Portrait Gallery; ch 61: Michael D. Beckwith/Wiki Commons; ch 68: Image courtesy of the dean and chapter, Westminster Abbey; ch 90: Karin Tearle, image courtesy of the parochial church council of St Paul's Cathedral; ch 90: Karin Tearle, by permission of Strawberry Hill House and Garden; ch 94: Karin Tearle, courtesy of Inner and Middle Temple

Terry Philpot was born within the sound of Bow Bells (which are not in the East End). He is a writer and award-winning journalist. He has written and edited more than 20 books ranging from social history to social policy. He has contributed to *The Times*, *The Guardian*, *The Daily Telegraph* and other publications. He is author of 25 entries for the *Oxford Dictionary of National Biography.* He has been a trustee of several charities and a co-founder of the One World Group. He worked with prisoners on Death Row in the USA and is a volunteer for New Bridge, which works with UK prisoners. He is a volunteer guide with the Wiener Holocaust Library.

Karin Tearle has a BA in French and Italian from Goldsmiths, University of London and lived in Bordeaux, France for several years before returning to the UK to have a family. She is a trustee of the Rwanda Development Trust which funds small capacity-building projects and was interpreter for the BBC World Service for a programme about the 1994 genocide. Karin has retained her links with the country and continues to work with the Rwandese. She also manages a listed building in Greenwich and has an affinity with this historic town where she has lived for thirteen years. Karin is social secretary of Aperture Woolwich Photographic Society, one of the oldest clubs in the country and is extremely passionate about photography.

The information in this book was accurate at the time of publication, but it can change at any time. Please confirm the details for the places you're planning to visit before you head out on your adventures.